PROSPECT WITH SOUL™
for Real Estate Agents

JENNIFER ALLAN-HAGEDORN

Bluegreen Books
publisher@bluegreenbooks.com

ISBN: 978-0-9816727-4-8

Edited by Barbara Munson, Munson Communications,
www.MunsonCommunications.com
Index by Madge Walls, All Sky Indexing, www.allskyindexing.com
Cover design by Sheryl Evans, Evans Studios, www.evans-studios.com
Interior design by: Jonathan Gullery, RJ Communications, www.booksjustbooks.com

First Printing 2011

Printed in the United States of America

CONTENTS

Dedication

To my Super Bruce... I've been asked if having you in my life has made a difference in my writing career. In a word (okay, 3 words)—oh, my, YES! No question, my business (not to mention my life) has improved exponentially since you came along. I'll be eternally grateful (as in, 'til death do us part) for the support and enthusiasm you've shown for my work, and of course, all the love you've shown to me and my livestock. I'm the luckiest Bwajah in the whole world—the universe even!

And Jed, thanks for hogging the TV, thus banishing me to the office, forcing me to <gasp> work all day and finish this book in record time.

This one's for my new family—love y'all!

The Story of Joe

AS TOLD TO THE AUTHOR
BY DENNIS J. GIANNETTI

Joe was at a crossroads in his real estate career.

Business was okay…not great by any means, but it paid the bills, most months anyway. Joe couldn't really complain since many of his associates had no idea where their next mortgage payment was coming from and more than a few were on the verge of leaving the business altogether.

While Joe hadn't reached that point, he frequently felt discouraged and wasn't having nearly as much fun selling real estate as he'd had in the past. In fact, lately he'd had to drag himself into the office to do the three hours of focused prospecting his new coach recommended. He usually spent these hours calling expired listings and FSBOs, with occasional calls to friends to remind them to send referrals his way.

Even though Joe didn't really enjoy all this focused prospecting, he knew it had to be done. Especially in today's market, where buyers and sellers weren't found on every street corner, it was even more necessary than it had been in years past to devote a significant amount of time and energy to prospecting for new business.

So, as much as Joe dreaded his daily three-hour prospecting routine, he told himself that the end goal was worth the pain—that eventually he'd have a more consistent stream of business coming in the door and then he wouldn't have to worry so much about where his next client would come from.

Because he did worry a lot about that. Some days the worry consumed him, to the point where he couldn't think about anything else. He knew the stress was

2   Prospect with Soul for Real Estate Agents

affecting his business and his health, not to mention his marriage, and that he needed to make a change.

But...what?

One day, instead of going in to the office at 8:00 a.m. as was his habit, he found himself driving to the beach, almost as if a force beyond his control was steering the car.

When he arrived, there was no one else there. Well, almost no one. Standing along the water's edge, amidst the waves crashing into the shore, was a woman moving in place, slowly, with grace and fluidity. To Joe, it was almost as if she were one with the ocean. She seemed completely at peace and, in a moment of clarity, Joe realized that more than anything else, he too wanted that peace. He waited patiently for the woman to complete the exercise and, as she headed toward the steps leaving the beach, Joe hesitantly waved at her.

"Sorry, can I ask what you were doing out there?"

"Sure," she answered, "I was doing a little moving meditation. Is it something you want to learn?"

"Um, not really," Joe admitted. He paused. "But I would really love to be at peace like that--you know focused, flowing, clear."

"I see," said the woman. "May I ask why you don't have this feeling now?"

"That's the thing," said Joe, "I don't really know."

"Well, I have some time this morning. Would you like to join me for a cup of tea and talk about it?"

About 10 minutes later, they were sitting in a small café.

Joe asked the woman what she did for a living.

"Oh, I'm retired now, but I was a real estate agent for years," the woman responded.

It was like music to Joe's ears. Could this woman hold the answers to his questions?

As the woman took her first sip of peppermint tea, Joe told her he also was a real estate agent.

"Ah," said the woman, "and that is where your confusion is coming from?"

The woman's soft voice and calm demeanor opened the floodgates for Joe. For over an hour, he poured out his frustrations and fears, his hopes and dreams. The woman listened quietly, occasionally taking notes on her napkin.

When Joe ran out of steam, he smiled sheepishly and apologized for monopolizing the conversation.

"Not at all," the woman assured him. "I have to go now, but I'd like to meet you again. I think I can help you find what you're looking for. Meet me at the beach tomorrow morning and I will share with you how what you saw me doing on the beach today relates to what you need to do to change your business."

"Can't wait," Joe said sincerely.

The next morning, Joe arrived at the beach and found the woman already there, in movement as she'd been the morning before. Fluid, purposeful, and peaceful. In a few minutes, she concluded her exercise and smiled at Joe.

"Ready?" she asked.

"Absolutely," answered Joe.

"Tell me, what was I doing just then?"

"Um, meditating? Tai chi?" Joe guessed.

"That's what it's called, but what was I *doing*?"

Pausing for a moment, Joe took a shot at going deep. "Um, connecting? Becoming one with your environment? Finding yourself from the inside out?"

The woman laughed softly. "Close enough, Joe, close enough. Now, let me ask you this—when you're prospecting, do you feel any of those things? Do you feel connected? Are you acting in a way that makes you peaceful from the inside out?"

"Well, no," Joe admitted, "but I'm just doing what I was taught. Is that wrong?"

"Does it feel right?"

"Well, to be honest, no," Joe answered.

"Why not?"

Joe paused.

"I feel like…I feel like I'm pushing people to do things they don't want to do. Like I'm trying to be someone I'm not in order to make things happen."

"Go on," said the woman.

"Well, I don't know how to explain it, but you know how you move so gracefully and effortlessly on the beach? I feel nothing like that day to day. I feel like I'm stumbling on my own efforts. I'm not excited about what I do anymore, or how I do it."

"I see," said the woman. "So, what do you think would make you feel more at peace? What do you want to change?"

"I want…I want to feel that I'm bringing real value to my clients. I want to feel confident when I prospect that I'm truly the best man for the job, not just a man who needs a paycheck. I want the people I know to think of me as an exceptional real estate agent who is deserving of their business and referrals. I want to build a successful real estate business without, well, without selling my soul, if you know what I mean."

"Excellent," said the woman. "Now here's the good news. Everything you say you want; everything you are seeking, is within your reach. It's already inside you. The problem is that you are ignoring your own quiet voice and, instead, you're listening to all those louder, more insistent voices on the outside telling you to do it their way. That emptiness and confusion you feel is just your soul trying to get your attention.

"Sounds kind of new-agey," Joe protested, but without conviction.

"Maybe," agreed the woman. "But it's true. To experience the success you dream of, you need to be in touch with who you are. You need to let *who you are* define *what you do*, not *what you do* define *who you are*."

"Wow," said Joe. "That makes sense. I think it does, anyway."

The woman smiled and continued. "Let's end today's lesson this way. You have been working for a commission check. You are attached to the outcome. But you feel empty inside. You seek to fill that emptiness by pursuing more and bigger commission checks. But the reality is that a commission check is simply the reward for doing a great job, not a definition of who you are. If you want to increase the balance in your bank account and your life, you need to listen to your soul and trust what it is telling you."

Joe took a moment to ponder this.

"Ok," he said. "I'm in. What do I have to do?"

"Meet me tomorrow, same place, same time. I will show you how to find people to serve and provide value to. I will teach you how to prospect from the inside out."

"Kind of like prospecting with soul," Joe said, trying to be witty.

"Exactly," said the woman. "Now, go enjoy your day. I'll see you tomorrow."

> "Always be a first-rate version of yourself, instead of
> a second-rate version of somebody else."
> —Judy Garland

CHAPTER ONE

Welcome to Prospect with Soul™

FORGET everything you've ever heard or read about effective real estate prospecting techniques. If those ideas and advice had worked for you, you probably wouldn't be holding this book in your hands right now. When we've finished our journey together, you are welcome to return to your old ways of building your business…or join us Soulful Prospectors who have found a better way.

A better way to what, exactly? Ah, glad you asked. A better way to inspire the people you know and the people you meet to think of you as their favorite real estate agent. A way to attract business to you without pestering anyone or jeopardizing the personal relationships in your life. A way to be wildly successful without sacrificing your soul (or your dignity) in the process.

A way to use the brains God gave you to build a thriving business you'll be proud to call your own. One that will pay the bills nicely, while leaving you time to enjoy the lifestyle you've always dreamed your prospecting efforts would eventually result in.

A way to, get this, NEVER HAVE TO PROSPECT AGAIN!

This is the ultimate goal of building a career by Prospecting with Soul…to have generated the good will, the respect, the recognition and the reputation to NEVER HAVE TO PROSPECT AGAIN!

Well, maybe that's stretching it just a bit. As an entrepreneurial sort, you'll always have to ensure a steady stream of business to your door to keep the dogs fed and the toenails polished. And yes, attracting business your way will require some effort on your part. However, by the time we're finished with you here at the Prospect with Soul Worldwide headquarters, you'll be comfortably prospecting as a natural part of your day-to-day wanderings, without even realizing you're doing it. So, yeah, you're prospecting, but it's almost as natural as breathing.

About Sell with Soul™ (SWS)

If this is your first encounter with all this real estate "Soul" stuff, you might be wondering what it's all about!

Sell with Soul is the name of my first book and the basis for my entire real estate philosophy. Since we'll be referring to SWS here and there throughout this book, here's a little primer on what it means.

Sell with Soul: To enjoy a wildly successful career selling real estate by treating clients and prospects respectfully, as you yourself would like to be treated.

Sounds suspiciously like the good old Golden Rule of doing unto others what you would like them to do unto you, doesn't it? Which, by the way, you'll see as a common theme in *Prospect with Soul*.

An agent who Sells with Soul wants to earn the future business and referrals of his satisfied past clients because he is the best agent to have ever happened to them—not because he masters the art of referral-begging (see Chapter Four—Your Sphere of Influence). Because he's so darn good at what he does, eventually he won't have to prospect at all—with soul or otherwise—because his satisfied past clients will do it for him. Seriously.

To Sell with Soul also means that you respect and appreciate your clients, and therefore do not use tricks or strategies that are insulting or patronizing to them. SWS agents respect the intelligence of their clients and prospects and treat them accordingly. They don't insult that intelligence with ridiculous scripts, pushy closing techniques or cheesy objection-busters. They are patient and kind. Empathetic and sympathetic. Respectful and appreciative.

SWS'ers (real estate agents who follow Sell with Soul principles) strive to place their clients in first position, where they belong, rather than lower on the priority totem pole to be dealt with after one's prospecting is done. When an SWS'er is faced with a dilemma, he first considers the wants and needs of the client and makes his decision accordingly.

An agent who Sells with Soul wants to be competent before he sets himself loose on the general public. He believes that anyone who honors him with their business deserves more than a "fake it 'til you make it" attitude. He thinks it only fair that he is qualified and competent before he asks for and accepts payment for his professional expertise.

An SWS'er can, with a straight face and sincere heart, make the following two statements:

1. "The clients I have today are more important to me than the clients I hope to have tomorrow."
2. "I am, or intend to be, the best thing to ever happen to my client."

Then, What Does It Mean to Prospect with Soul...or, Conversely, withOUT Soul?

Let's go back to that definition of Sell(ing) with Soul—something about making lots of money selling real estate by treating people the way you'd like to be treated, right?

Therefore, the definition of Prospect(ing) with Soul might read something like this: "To build a real estate business using techniques and strategies that: 1) you're proud of and excited about, 2) would work if used on you, and 3) don't make you feel icky."

So, let's look at the elements of that definition one by one.

"To use techniques and strategies that you're proud of and excited about"

So many agents, particularly newer ones, get sucked into prospecting programs, systems and methods that they're embarrassed by and certainly not excited about. It's as if they assume that somehow they'll be changed into a different person— someone who tomorrow will embrace ideas that seem silly and cheesy today—all because they've written a check or hired a coach. Even as their common sense whispers to them that the approach they're contemplating is wrong (for them), they insist on giving it a try, just in case they're wrong about being wrong!

No, no, no! Before implementing any prospecting strategy, be darn sure that it's something you're jazzed up, revved up and fired up to do. And not because some guru promised you the earth, moon and stars if you'll just sign on the dotted line and turn over a chunk of your precious marketing budget. And never forget that only you can make the determination whether you should be proud of and excited about something; no one else can (or should) do that for you.

"To use techniques and strategies that would work on you"

Why, oh why do we real estate agents insist on implementing prospecting techniques that wouldn't work on us in a million years? Do we really think our audience is that much different from us (or dumber than we are) that they will react positively to something we wouldn't give the time of day to?

Oh, I know why we do it. Our brokers and trainers and associates swear by the techniques and tell us to "just give it a try." We don't have enough faith in our own gut instincts, so we give in. We'll talk more about this later.

"To use techniques and strategies that don't make you feel icky"

Why do we real estate agents insist on implementing prospecting techniques that make us feel icky? That give us the willies? That make our guts churn, our noses wrinkle and our eyes roll? This is the epitome of NOT Prospecting with Soul— to do unto others what would annoy us if done unto us.

Feeling icky about any activity should be a clear indication that there's something wrong with the activity (for you). But, as with strategies that wouldn't work on you if used on you, your brokers and trainers and associates tell you that what you're really feeling is fear, not ickiness. That if you can just suck it up, get out of your comfort zone and Do It (whatever that "it" is you don't want to do), you'll eventually get over those feelings of ick and even enjoy the activity.

But there's a big difference between being reasonably nervous about something you haven't done before and feeling icky about it. Your gut knows the difference. Trust it.

And again, we'll talk more about this later.

One more thing to toss in here about evaluating a prospecting strategy—never implement a strategy that insults the intelligence of your target audience.

It seems obvious that, when looking for business, you don't want to imply you think your audience is stupid. Most people in the world have a high regard for their own intelligence (whether deserved or not), so when your self-promotional materials take the tone of a lofty, smarter-than-thou know-it-all OR of a cheesy, patronizing huckster, your audience will react in one of two ways (neither one positive).

One, they might be insulted by your insinuation that you're smarter than they are or, two, they might think less of your intelligence level since your marketing material clearly demonstrates, um, a LACK of intelligence. What they won't think is how awesome you are, how worthy of their business you are, or how much they respect your abilities as a real estate agent.

***

Here's a quote from one of my favorite books on the planet—*Go-Givers Sell More* by Bob Burg and John David Mann:

"You may have been taught that to be successful in sales, you need to 'step outside your comfort zone.' Let's reexamine that idea. If you push yourself to a place that makes you uncomfortable, chances are pretty good you'll end up making the other person uncomfortable, too. Consciously or not, they'll sense your discomfort—and attitudes are contagious.

We human beings tend to resist discomfort; in fact, we'll typically do anything to avoid putting ourselves in uncomfortable situations. Why base your entire career on something your strongest instincts tell you to avoid?"

When you Prospect with Soul, you're proud of and excited about your prospecting efforts. You don't feel the need to apologize for, explain or defend them. You can't wait to implement your latest approach and are looking forward to feedback from your audience. You have no real doubt that your audience will be receptive and responsive to your prospecting; in fact, you're pretty sure they'll get a kick out of it.

That's how you know it's right. When you're excited about it. When you're proud of it.

Oh, sure, you might have a moment or two of self-doubt, of trepidation, of insecurity. After all, you're doing something that could directly contradict everything you've ever heard about effective prospecting. You're probably being more transparent and authentic than you've been before. (And not spending nearly as much money on your prospecting as you thought you had to.)

If you ever find yourself not sure whether what you're feeling is fear or ick, run the prospecting approach you're contemplating thru these three "tests" and see if it qualifies as Prospecting with Soul…or not:

1. Are you proud of and excited about this approach?
2. Would it work on you?
3. Does it make you feel icky?

If you answer "yes" to 1) and 2), and "no" to 3), you're just a little nervous about trying something new. But if your contemplated approach fails any of the tests, it's back to the drawing board for you! And that's a good thing, as you will see.

In the chapters that follow, you'll learn about many real estate prospecting techniques that have been used successfully by agents who follow the philosophies of Selling with Soul. But that doesn't mean that every technique described here is right for you. In fact, it's likely that a few will fail the test miserably—**for you.**

Again, trust that gut of yours. It knows what it's talking about.

The Old School

In *Sell with Soul*, I describe The Old School as the real estate trainers, authors, brokers, mentors and coaches who encourage—heck, celebrate—decidedly UNsoulful prospecting techniques. Techniques that any reasonably intelligent prospect can see through and any real estate agent with a modicum of self-respect should be too embarrassed to apply.

What are some examples of Old School techniques? Well, the obvious ones are cold-calling and door-knocking, of course. I will never, ever encourage a real estate agent to do either of these activities; I don't care if they "work" or not. We don't approve of such activities in these parts—anything that will annoy the masses in hopes of capturing the few just doesn't fly in PWSLand.

The other Old School technique I won't have in my house is Referral-Begging. We'll talk more about this, and what to do instead, in Chapter Four.

Old School techniques center on treating your real estate career like a Numbers Game. Where the goal is to assault as many people as you can with your sales-pitch, without consideration for whether or not these people appreciate being assaulted with your sales-pitch. The Old School believes that the end justifies the means. At the end of the day, they say, if your annoying activities result in business for you, then all is right with the world.

What to Expect from This Book

In short, expect to experience a massive paradigm shift, if you've been frustrated so far in your real estate prospecting efforts. What you will read may sound completely nonsensical, counterintuitive or even nuts if you've been brainwashed by the vast majority of the real estate sales training material out there.

However, those of you to whom the Prospecting with Soul philosophy comes naturally will almost certainly discover some new prospecting ideas that will be oh-so doable for you and your personality.

Does the End Justify the Means?

A few years ago, I went on a cruise to the Bahamas. Even though I was sternly warned that I would not work on vacation, I couldn't help but notice all sorts of analogies between my cruising experience and the wonderful world of real estate sales.

I remember following a conversation on a real estate forum about call-capture. Whether or not to do it. Whether or not it annoys people who get a call out of nowhere from a stranger. **Whether or not it matters if you annoy people**. The consensus was that it does not matter if people are annoyed by an unsolicited phone call; if the strategy works every once in a while, it's worth the annoyance imposed.

Frankly, that seems to be the mantra of the Old School traditional real estate model.

Anyway, back to my cruise vacation. As we got on the cruise ship after a 7-hour drive, we were bombarded with lights, music and activity. Selling activity. We were offered a Welcome Bahama Mama (for $8.95+tip). A few steps away was a booth selling soda packages ($29.00 for all the soda you can drink PLUS a free insulated cup!). To the side was a guy hawking on-shore excursions. To the other side was a young woman promoting an on-board detoxification experience in the spa.

Being the introvert that I am, I just wanted to escape to my room for a moment of silence. The joy I felt at finally being On Vacation was a little dampened by all the attention focused on getting into my pocketbook. But was the approach working? Oh, yeah, there were people lined up at every booth, brand-spanking new SeaPass card in hand, ready to start spending their dollars within minutes of boarding.

A few days later, I found myself disembarking into Nassau. If you've ever been to Nassau, you know what happened next. We were accosted by local dudes offering buggy rides, scooters, taxis, hair-braiding (okay, those were women), snorkel trips... along with plenty of offers for less-legal products. None of which we bought, by the way. But that didn't stop them—we spent the day fending off sales pitches and requests for tips from people we'd never seen before and pushing away "free" bracelets and trinkets.

Now, do these people really think anyone appreciates their approach? That their visitors enjoy the experience of being incessantly accosted on their vacation? I can't imagine they do, but, it's worth it because it results in sales.

Does the end justify the means in marketing? If you believe it does, how do you convince yourself that it's okay to do unto others that which would annoy the hell out of you if done unto you?

So, what have you gotten yourself into here? Do I really expect you to believe that you can succeed in a real estate career without doing anything that pushes you out of your comfort zone or makes you feel icky?

Yes. Believe it. And let's get to it.

What You Won't Find in This Book

Prospect with Soul is not just another book about prospecting for real estate business. It's about building a real estate business without selling your soul to do it. Therefore, in the interest of staying on point, I made the executive decision to exclude some of the more basic details of various prospecting methods, assuming (hopefully safely) that you can find these details elsewhere. Attention spans are short (yours AND mine!), so I chose to focus on material you'll likely not find anywhere else.

Therefore, as you read the chapter about Open Houses, for example, you won't find anything about effective sign placement or newspaper announcements. Nothing much about home brochures. Nothing at all about what sorts of cookies to bring or beverages to offer.

Nor will you find material that I already covered in my other books. Where appropriate, I'll refer you to those books and you can decide if you want to invest in them (or dig out your already-owned copies to review!).

Because I want you to create your own real estate business, one you're proud of and can maintain over the long term, you won't find a lot of structured processes or strict protocols to follow. Nor will you see formal scripts to memorize and recite. My hope in offering *Prospect with Soul* is to inspire you to think outside the proverbial box, to embrace what is naturally wonderful about you and to reject conventional wisdom if it doesn't sound all that wise to you!

If you've bought into the idea that you have to spend a fortune on advertising, pester strangers and even your friends for business, beg everyone you know for referrals and subject strangers to your sales pitch at every opportunity, accepting what I'm about to share with you may require a fairly significant shift in your mindset. Or…maybe not. Frankly, most people who are attracted to the Prospecting with Soul philosophy get it right away—and wonder how on earth they missed something so obvious.

"Believe nothing, no matter where you read it, or who said it,
no matter if I have said it, unless it agrees with your
own reason and your own common sense."
—Buddha

CHAPTER TWO

Choosing the Right
Prospecting Strategies for You

THIS book will present several prospecting strategies for you to consider,
evaluate and accept, reject or tweak to your liking.

Did you get that? I fully expect you to reject some of the strategies presented,
without even trying them!

I'm not one of those sales trainers who encourages her students to "try everything
at least once" to see how they like it. Hey, I trust you. You're an adult human
being with a good head on her shoulders, fully capable of making her own judgments and decisions as to how best to pursue business for herself. If something
you read here is of absolutely no interest to you, you have my blessing to wrinkle
your nose and skip to the next chapter.

That said, I also fully expect a few of the strategies will speak to your soul. Will
give you a sense of calm and peace, yet fill you with the excitement that, yes, you
can do this!

The rest of the strategies presented will fall somewhere in between. They don't
make you feel icky, and you recognize that you could do them, but they don't

inspire you to run right out and get started. These are the strategies you'll either tweak to better suit your personality and business model or backburner for times when you're feeling the need to expand your prospecting efforts.

I Trust You. Do You Trust You?

The very first lesson I want you to take away from this book is that I think you should trust you. Trust your instincts. Listen to your gut. Believe your heart. Acknowledge that you are an intelligent, capable, competent adult human being with reasonably good judgment and a fair share of common sense. I trust you…and I want you to trust you, too.

"Sure, Jennifer, that's very sweet, but what if I feel I don't have good sense, that I don't make wise decisions, that I can't be trusted to take care of the important issues in life? What if my history demonstrates a consistent pattern of, well, screwing everything up?"

Hey, I've been there and I've felt those feelings. I've made my share of mistakes and done some really stupid things, hoping I was onto something good. But you know what? Almost every single time I've messed up bad, I knew in my gut that what I was doing was wrong. Oh, not necessarily morally wrong (although I might have ventured there once or twice, shhhhh), but rather, I talked myself into doing something that didn't feel comfortable. Better said, I let someone else convince me it was a good idea even though it sounded silly or counterintuitive to me. But, I figured, hey, this person surely knows more than I do, so I'll just disregard my gut and take a chance.

Unfortunately, darn near every time I've disregarded my gut, I've regretted it.

At the ripe old age of 44, I'm finally learning that my gut knows what it's talking about. It knows what's right for me. I finally trust my own instincts, even when they conflict mightily with "common knowledge" or "industry standard."

For example, do you know what a "sales letter" is, from an online marketing perspective? You've probably seen a hundred of them. They're sort of the television infomercials for marketing on the web.

Prospecting—If It Feels Wrong, DON'T Do It!

One fine day last spring, I got a phone call from a real estate agent whose name didn't ring a bell. This agent whose name didn't ring a bell small-talked with me for a few minutes while I racked my brain to figure out if he was someone I should remember.

When the small-talking was done, he asked me if I knew anyone moving to his town that I could refer to him. Ahhhhhh, sez Jennifer, now I get it. He's prospecting. Well, I didn't happen to know anyone moving to his area, so I asked him to send me an email with his contact information and I'd be glad to keep him in mind. He bade me farewell and hung up. And I never heard from him.

I thought it was pretty funny—cold-calling someone and asking for referrals—and then not even following up? Interesting strategy. But over the next month, I got more such calls from agents around the country, all asking me if I knew anyone moving to their area.

I gently tried to dissuade the callers from making more such calls to their spheres of influence, but they all seemed determined and even enthusiastic about their phone calls.

Well, okay. To each his or her own. Far be it from me to talk someone out of a prospecting technique they're excited about.

It finally dawned on me that these calls must be part of a corporate training program. My assumption was correct—there was a program making the rounds where participants were instructed to call 100 people per week and ask for referrals.

Whatever. I think it's a ridiculous strategy to abuse friendships with any sort of referral-begging, but I know I'm in the minority in the world of real estate training.

The epilogue to this story is that I heard from one of the agents again the other day. Was she calling to hit me up again for referrals to her area? Nope. She was calling to apologize for doing it the first time. That she'd felt sick to her stomach doing it, not only to me, but to the other dozens of friends and acquaintances she subjected her pitch to. She is concerned that she'd actually damaged her friendships so she asked for advice on how to repair that damage.

My friends, if it feels wrong DON'T DO IT. IGNORE the well-intentioned(?) coaches and trainers and brokers who tell you to venture out of your comfort zone in order to succeed. Because there's a difference between overcoming a fear of something new and doing something you feel is wrong. A BIG difference. And you know what? You can tell the difference if you'll only pay attention to that little voice inside of you. It knows what it's talking about!

Basically a sales letter is a promotional piece for a product or service that follows a rather specific formula of building interest, creating urgency, providing testimonials and then initiating a compelling call-to-action.

So, several years ago, I was frustrated with the sales of my training products. Naturally, I jumped online and searched for "online marketing techniques." Read all about the incredibly effective "sales letter." I found a site that offered 101 sample sales letters for $29.99 and another that promised (for $4,200) to teach me to make a million dollars writing sales letters for myself and others. Of course, I also found links to dozens of professional sales letter writers (who probably took the $4,200 course) who could help me write my letter for just $500.

I coughed up the $29.99 for the 101 sample letters. Tried to read through them, but after four or five I was laughing hysterically. Were they serious? Could this garbage possibly work on anyone with two brain cells to knock together?

But, truth be told, I was a little desperate at the time and choked back my skepticism. I decided that even if the approach didn't sit well with me, it was worth trying if it would improve my sales. I called three of the sales letter professional writers I found online. Thankfully, all three were booked up for a few months, so I back-burnered the project indefinitely. In retrospect, I now know that I would have been mortified to have one of those cheesy letters on my website, representing me and my philosophies, but in my desperation to solve the problem, I was tempted to ignore my gut.

I'm glad I didn't.

Here's another example of gut-trusting I'm sure you can relate to. Early in my real estate career, my broker advised me to send out a cheesy announcement to all my friends announcing my venture into real estate. He showed me a sample announcement and I was underwhelmed. It was a pre-printed tri-fold brochure that raved about "the agent whose business card is enclosed"—how professional, well-trained and caring "I" was, and how I had the support of one of the most successful real estate companies in the country. Or something like that. I immediately pictured myself getting such an announcement from a friend and, in my mind's eye, watched myself toss it into the trash without a second thought! But, my broker swore it was the Thing to Do, so I did it. Wasted several hundred bucks in printing and postage, and didn't get so much as a phone call from any of the 182 lucky recipients.

I should have trusted my gut.

I have a hundred of these stories and I'm sure you do, too. So, promise me, from here on out, before spending any money, time or energy on a prospecting project, that you'll ask your gut how it feels about it. And listen.

Please Note

Throughout this book, I'm going to give you advice from my own experience and expertise. I'll make suggestions and provide direction. But guess what? Just because I say it doesn't mean it's 100% right for you! Yep, promise me that you'll check with your gut before implementing any of the strategies I'm going to share with you to see if they're a fit for you. If not, you have my blessing to reject them, change them or improve them to the point where they feel right. But when making such judgments, make sure you're listening to your own quiet voice, not those louder, more insistent voices around you.

Promise me.

One Last Thought Before We Begin: Systems

In the real estate industry, any product that promises a sure-fire system or comprehensive toolkit or strict procedure to follow has a great chance of success... success selling a lot of the product, that is.

We real estate agents love a good system. Or, rather, we love a system that promises results regardless of whether it's any good. There are door-knocking systems, Expired Listing systems, For-Sale-By-Owner systems, direct-mail systems, email newsletter systems, greeting card systems...all promising that if the agent simply commits to the system and works it hard, he'll see measurable and predictable results.

Fair enough.

Of course, most agents can't or won't follow the system 100% all the time, for various reasons, and when the system doesn't produce the results they desire, they "have no one to blame but themselves," right? Had they just worked harder, they'd be deliriously satisfied with their investment into the system.

So what's my point? To disclose, right up front, that if you're hoping to find a streamlined system for building your business in this book, you might want to see if you can get your money back. The Prospect with Soul approach is not a point-n-shoot, click-n-drag or one-size-fits-most magic bullet; no, it's all about creating a product and a message you're so darn proud of so you can't help but enthusiastically deliver it to the world.

STOP the Insanity! If What You're Doing Isn't Working, Try Something Different!

It's funny how we human beings think. If we're told by an "expert" to do something a certain way...and we do it...and it doesn't work for us, what do we do? Try something else? Nope. We do "it" (whatever "it" is) MORE.

For example, let's say your doctor tells you that in order to lose weight you need to eat less fat. You obey.

You feel crummy, you're hungry all the time and you're not losing weight, so you figure..."Hmmmm, I must not be cutting out ENOUGH fat." So you eat even less fat, you feel worse, you're even hungrier and you're still not losing weight, so what do you do? Blame yourself. You aren't doing ENOUGH of what you were told to do. You suck as a human being. You're an utter failure.

Same thing with selling real estate. We're trained to cold-call, door-knock, advertise, farm, pester our friends for referrals and create a killer website. When these prospecting approaches don't work, we're advised to do it MORE. "You aren't calling ENOUGH strangers, you aren't sending out ENOUGH postcards, you aren't annoying your friends often ENOUGH, you need to spend even MORE money on your website."

I call BS.

If something isn't working, why not try something ELSE? Sure, there's honor (and some wisdom) in being persistent and patient, but I think we're all smart enough to know when something ain't right for us. If you're eating low-fat and you feel crummy (and you're still fat), try low-carb. If that doesn't work, try raw. If that doesn't work...try something ELSE.

Find what works for you. Find what's fun for you. Find what makes you smile and feel GOOD about getting up in the morning. Because I can promise you, blindly following the crowd in our business is crazy...when you consider that the vast majority of that crowd is failing...

Many faithful readers of my books and blog lean toward the introverted end of the personality spectrum. Not all do, of course, but more than you might think given that the traditional view of a career in real estate sales assumes a certain level of people-person-ness.

Being an introvert myself, I can't let a book of mine get published without a few words celebrating the wonderfulness of the introverted real estate agent. If you don't consider yourself to be an introvert, you may skip this section... or perhaps keep reading. You might be surprised at how much you identify with the introverted personality! Throughout this book, you'll see callouts specifically speaking to my introverted readers. Again, if you don't consider yourself an introvert, you're free to pass 'em on by.

"I'm an Introvert."

Now before you smile sympathetically and congratulate me for the courage it took to confess to my introversion, be assured that I'm proud of my personality! I like who I am and make no apologies. There's nothing wrong with being an introvert; in fact, there's a whole lot right about it. Contrary to popular belief, we introverts are not always shy or withdrawn or unfriendly, although we've lived our lives thinking we are. We're creative...intelligent...thoughtful...empathetic... imaginative. We're organized, efficient and reliable. We do what we say we're going to do, when we say we're going to do it. We have the ability and desire to put ourselves in the other fellow's shoes and see things from their perspective.

Doesn't this sound like someone **you'd** like to have managing your real estate transaction?

Introvert vs. Extrovert

An Extrovert is someone who gets his or her energy from being around others; an Introvert is someone who is energized by being alone. When an Extrovert is left alone for long periods of time, he becomes lethargic. Conversely, an Introvert will be exhausted and drained after a day of social interaction.

Are All Soulful Prospectors Introverts?

No. Just because you don't relish the thought of aggressively prospecting for business doesn't make you an introvert. I have a lot of extroverted friends who embrace the tenets of Soulful Prospecting, even though they are naturally outgoing, charismatic and socially comfortable. Granted, many of my readers find me via my writing on the Introvert experience. Maybe you did, too. So I think it's safe to say that an awful lot of Soulful Prospectors ARE Introverts. But if you aren't, don't worry; this book does not assume that you are.

"But You Don't ACT Shy!"

I hear this a lot. When I tell someone I'm an introvert, they immediately equate it with being shy. I, myself, used the terms interchangeably in my first book, and later realized that they really weren't the same thing.

Marti Olsen Laney, Psy.D., in *The Introvert Advantage*, describes introversion and shyness as follows:

"Introversion: This is a healthy capacity to tune into your inner world. It is a constructive and creative quality that is found in many independent thinkers whose contributions have enriched the world. Introverts have social skills, they like people, and they enjoy some types of socializing. However, party chitchat depletes their energy while giving them little in return. Introverts enjoy one-on-one conversations, but group activities can be over-stimulating and drain energy.

Shyness: Shyness is social anxiety, an extreme self-consciousness when one is around people. It may have some genetic roots, but it is usually learned from experiences at school, with friends and in families…Shy people may feel uncomfortable with one-on-one conversations or in group situations. It is not an issue of energy; it is a lack of confidence in social situations. It is a fear of what others think of you."

Why is this distinction important? Well, because if someone is truly shy, as opposed to introverted, they may not be suited to the life of a real estate agent. Just something to think about.

[By the way, if you consider yourself an introvert at all, I'll save you a whole bunch of money right here and now. I'll bet you get bombarded with advertisements for glitzy seminars promising to double your business, and many of them look pretty darn sexy, don't they? 100% Money Back Guarantee! What do you have to lose? Well, only your time, your energy, your enthusiasm and very likely, your money, even with that unconditional guarantee.

These programs won't work for you. They're created by and for extroverts—for the belly-to-belly type salespeople who enjoy nothing more than a good afternoon of cold-calling or evening of hearty back-slapping, card-swapping networking. If just the thought of such activities makes you long to crawl under the covers, then you have much better places to spend your time and your money.]

"Money is usually attracted, not pursued."
—Jim Rohn

Chapter Three

Don't Pursue, Attract!

As a real estate agent who must ensure a steady stream of clients for herself, you have two big-picture options as to how to go about getting those clients to your door.

Option One: You can go out and get them, or

Option Two: You can attract them to you.

Let me guess which option sounds more "attractive" to you…hmmmm…I'll bet Option Two is sounding pretty sweet. Well, guess what?! Option Two IS by far the best option for the Soulful Prospector! Not just because attracting business to you allows you to stay in your comfort zone, it also just plain works better!

It's true! What worked for real estate agents back in the dark ages, before the turn of the millennium, may not work today. What's different?

In a word—the Internet.

As I described in my last book, *If You're Not Having Fun Selling Real Estate, You're Not Doing it Right* (hereinafter referred to simply as "FUN"), the Internet has changed how consumers seek and obtain information. (*Duh, Jennifer, y'think?*). They no longer have to wait to be advertised to or rely on fluffed-up testimonials provided by the salesperson; no, they can go online and do all the research their hearts desire, including non-biased, objective opinions of whatever product or service they're considering purchasing.

Today's consumers are much less interested in being pitched to than they used to be, which, in all likelihood, they weren't much interested in back then, either.

So, the sales paradigms are shifting from a pursuit-oriented approach to an attraction-oriented one. Which is great news for us Soulful Prospectors.

I've found in my businesses—both as a real estate agent and as writer and trainer—that I'm a far more effective closer when my prospects approach me first. And when I say "far more effective" I mean, like 100 to one— that there's no comparison between my success rates when I make the first move versus when someone contacts me first.

If someone who wants to buy a home calls me from a For Sale sign in a yard, they're mine—no question. In that situation I'm a fantastic closer. However, if I contact, say, a real estate school and ask if they'd like to talk to me about teaching a class for them, they'll brush me off—99% of the time. Even if I offer to do it for free.

I don't know why this is—and if it's something I'm doing wrong or just the way of the world. Perhaps this is where the good old Numbers Game comes into play. You know the drill—how you have to contact so many potential prospects knowing only a small percentage will say yes, which by definition means a large percentage will say no. So, maybe if I called 100 real estate schools and pitched my services, I'd get in the door with two or three of them. But I promise you— that ain't gonna happen. I don't have the personality to handle all that rejection and if my career depended on pursuing that sort of rejection on a regular basis, I'd much rather be flipping burgers.

But back to our two options—going out and pursuing business, or attracting business to us.

Option One is sales in the traditional sense. You advertise, you self-promote, you network. Basically, you ask for business. But in today's increasingly noisy, chaotic and complicated world, it's getting harder to catch the attention of the buyer, who is already bombarded with dozens, maybe hundreds or even thousands of competing offers.

We consumers are getting good at tuning out all the noise. Seth Godin calls traditional advertising "Interruption Marketing." Which means pretty much what it sounds like—you must interrupt your potential customer from whatever he was doing to make your pitch, and hope he's in the mood to listen. Interestingly, Mr. Godin calls Interruption Marketers "hunters," which sounds to me like another name for "pursuers." And, in case you haven't read or heard Mr. Godin's opinion on the matter, he doesn't think much of Interruption Marketing as an effective tool to capture the attention of your target audience.

But whether or not Interruption Marketing is effective really doesn't matter to a Soulful Prospector. For us, traditional interruption marketing techniques are just plain uncomfortable. Not necessarily because we're shy or self-conscious or even insecure, no, we just don't do unto others what we don't want done unto us. And, the way we see it, no one really wants to be marketed to.

And that attitude colors our attempts at self-promotion. We apologize for disrupting or interrupting someone with our sales pitch, no matter how subtle. We dread our daily prospecting duties and question every dime spent on advertising. In short, we fear we're being a pest and it's likely our targets feel it, too.

Option Two, on the other hand, is very likely to become the 21st-century paradigm of prospecting. You create something that people want and they come to you to get it, or at least, to learn more about it. Your phone rings (or email jangles), you answer it (or open it) and voila! You have a great new client! Someone who is pursuing you, who wants what you have to offer, who is ready and willing to hear your sales pitch!

When potential customers seek you out (instead of the other way around), it gives you tremendous confidence. You might be surprised to find yourself standing a little straighter and speaking with more authority than you thought you had in you.

The trick of course, is to figure out how to create an attractive product and message that will bring potential homebuyers and sellers to you so you can work your magic.

So, let's talk about that.

Attracting Real Estate Business to You

In the real estate industry, business can come to you through a wide variety of sources. You can potentially get leads from:

- Your friends, family and acquaintances—*aka* your sphere of influence
- Strangers who see your name on a For Sale sign
- Open houses
- Your website
- Your blog
- Just being out there in the world with your antenna up
- Someone walks into or calls your office when you're on floor duty
- Your advertising
- Cold-calling
- A mass-mailing/farming campaign
- Just plain old good luck when someone stumbles onto your business card and gives you a call

With many of these lead types, you can choose either a pursuit-based or attraction-based approach. For example, with your sphere of influence, you can either call up everyone you know and ask them if they know anyone they can refer to you (pursuit), or you can simply strive to be an RCHB (RCHB—see Chapter Four) in their presence and inspire them to think of you as a kick-a$$ real estate agent (attract).

RCHB = Reasonably Competent Human Being

At an open house, we can aggressively ask each visitor if they already have a real estate agent and, if no, assault them with a sales pitch, or we can casually demonstrate our expertise in the local market and cheerfully answer any questions they may have. In your blog, you can deliver one blatant self-promotional article after another, or you can simply provide helpful, relevant, interesting information to your readers.

Some call attraction-based prospecting a passive approach and while I might argue with that semantically, there is some truth there. No, you don't sit at your desk and hope the phone rings—you are doing things that will make that phone ring, but those things don't include pursuing or interrupting people who have not expressed an interest in being pursued or interrupted.

It's all about how your audience wants to be prospected to. Today's consumer is growing weary of being pursued and is responding much more positively to attraction-based marketing.

Be assured that just because you prospect "passively" doesn't mean you have anything to apologize for. Create something people want, put it out there, and let them come to you.

As a result, your closing ratio, if you want to call it that, will likely be much higher than with pursuit-oriented prospecting because you're not disrupting someone with your message. They want what you have, so they seek you out, which gives you tremendous credibility with them from the start.

Yes, an attraction-based model IS more passive than the more traditional in-your-face marketing tactics, but that doesn't make it wrong. In fact, it might make it very, very right.

Reverse Psychology

Want to put someone on the defensive, fast? Say these two magic words: *"You should…"*

Have you ever noticed that your unsolicited advice to your friends, family, spouse or children is largely ignored or even resented? Irritating, isn't it? I mean, you know what they're doing wrong, what they should be doing instead and exactly how to help them get there—and they just don't appreciate it?!

Sheesh! Are we surrounded by ingrates?

Ummm. Well. Truth be told, I don't much like being told what to do, either, regardless of the good intentions of the tell-er. Any sentence that starts out with any semblance of the words "you should" is likely to result in a bristly response from me. Probably from you, too. Further, I can't say I much appreciate any helpful advice on how my character or behavior could use some improving, either. Might just spark an argument, in fact. Might? HA! It definitely will.

"Can I Get One of Your Business Cards?"

Ahhhh, music to a real estate agent's ears..."Can I have one of your business cards?" Or even better, "Do you have time to work with me?"

My regular readers know that I vehemently advise against accosting people you meet with your elevator speech or pushing your business card at every poor sap who happens to say hello to you at a party.

I believe with all my heart that if you believe with all your heart that you're a great real estate agent and if you love your job, that's enough to drive business to your door. No, I don't mean that you can sit on your sofa eating Twinkies and wait for clients to land in your lap; what I mean is that if you are confident in your abilities and enthusiastic about your career, that will be clear to the people you know and the people you meet...and they'll want some o'dat!

The trick to getting in the position to demonstrate your expertise and excitement is to subtly let people know you sell real estate for a living. If they're interested, they'll tell you. If they aren't...no biggie. Just talk about something else (y'know, like a "real" person would who isn't in prospecting mode).

Here's an example from my world.

Yesterday, I'm getting my toenails polished at a cute little Korean shop here in town. The toenail-polisher-guy tells me how he has to re-take his cosmetology exam because he accidently let his license expire. I laugh sympathetically and say, "Oh, I know what that's like, my real estate license expired a few years ago and it was a real pain to get it reactivated!" (That's not really true, but it seemed like a natural thing to say under the circumstances).

The woman sitting next to me immediately asks me if I sell real estate and I acknowledge that I do. We start talking about the real estate market, yada yada yada, and the next thing I know she's asking for my business card.

Why did she ask? Because I sales-pitched her into it? Nope. I guess I just sounded as if I knew what I was talking about and I didn't whine about the market. Maybe I even seemed like a pleasant person to do business with.

I can't remember the last time I offered someone my business card, but I get asked for it all the time. When you love what you do and you know you're good at it...you'll attract plenty of business your way...without ever asking for it. It's a beautiful way to make a living!

As a real estate agent, you want more business, right? Comes with the territory; even during those times where you're feeling overwhelmed and overworked, you know in the back of your mind that you should be looking for more.

Our natural inclination when we're on the prowl for business (or anything else we passionately want) is to come right out and ask for it. Demand it, even.

I remember when I was, *ahem*, much less mature than I am today, thinking that if I wanted someone to feel a certain way about me, I could bully him into it. I distinctly recall telling my boyfriend that he needed to decide soon if he wanted to take our relationship to the next level—which would include breaking up with his "other" girlfriend. I pushed and pushed, thinking I was being persuasive… and whaddya' know? He broke up with ME and stayed with HER. (Interesting epilogue to the story- a few months later she gave him her own ultimatum which drove him back to me.)

So, instead of telling people that they "should" hire you (or love you!), which will almost always put that person on the defensive, go ahead and give them permission not to.

Huh? Permission? Jennifer, what do you mean by that?

When you stop pushing, and even appear to be pulling away, it lets the other guy off the hook and allows him to make his own analysis of the situation without the distraction of feeling pushed or manipulated. And this can be a powerful prospecting tool, especially in the hands of a Soulful Prospector.

Here's an example I read last year. The gist of the article is that the author took his car to an oil change shop. They did their thing, but as they were doing their thing, they noticed that the guy's battery was low. So, they recommended that he replace the battery in the near future. And here's how they worded their recommendation: "*We highly recommend you change your battery soon. **Of course you'll want to shop around,** but we could put in the battery for you today.*"

The punch line to the story is that the author of the article did indeed purchase the battery from the oil change shop, acknowledging that their lack of obvious salesmanship was the key to winning his trust…and his business.

Of Course You'll Want to Shop Around

I had my vehicle's oil changed at Valvoline Instant Oil Change yesterday. There was a big banner in the shop that said something like, "We're Paid on Satisfaction, Not Commission." I noticed they had installed mirrors that allow customers who are sitting in their vehicles during the oil change to see what the mechanics are doing to their cars under their car hoods. Clearly, they are trying to make the oil change business more credible so that customers don't flinch when they find out about some additional work Valvoline recommends to their customers.

And I think the strategy is working. At least it worked for me. The tech ran a test on my battery, and the written report said it had a low charge. The report stated, "We highly recommend you change your battery soon."

The tech said, "Of course you'll want to shop around, but we could certainly put in a battery for you today."

I remembered there had been one day last winter when my car almost didn't start. That lingered in my memory. I told the tech I'd think about a new battery. And I did. And five minutes later, I was asking him how much a new battery would cost. And a minute after that, I was asking if he had one in stock. And a minute after that, the tech was installing a new battery in my vehicle.

Like many consumers, I'd become skeptical of auto repair facilities. Whenever a shop recommends work to be done, I wonder if I truly need the part or service being recommended. Since I know auto repair establishments have a rather poor reputation for recommending work that isn't really required, I usually avoid purchasing any of the add-ons that they propose to me.

But yesterday at Valvoline, my tech handled the situation perfectly. He did something I usually preach against: he recommended something, but he didn't ask for the sale. Yet, I made the purchase.

Sometimes reverse psychology works.

Skip is the Founder of Selling to Consumers Sales Training, www.sellingto-consumers.com

You can use a similar strategy in your real estate business. When you meet with a potential home seller who is interviewing several agents, ask who else they're talking to, if it seems like an appropriate question. If you know the other agent or agents, say something nice about them! The first time I used this strategy (unintentionally!)—I knew all of the other agents and they were all good. So I said that—I said, "*Well, all of those agents are good, so I think you'll be happy with whoever you select. Just pick the person you think is most excited about your house and who you can envision spending time with over the next few months.*"

Later, after I was hired, my seller told me that that statement was one of the deciding factors in her decision to hire me because every other agent put down the competition.

Your Elevator Speech

The last strategy I'm going to talk about to attract business to you is Your Elevator Speech. If you've ever done any sales training, you've no doubt heard of the infamous "elevator speech" or "elevator pitch."

The Elevator Speech

According to Wikipedia, an elevator pitch or speech is: "An overview of an idea for a product, service, or project. The name reflects the fact that an elevator pitch can be delivered in the time span of an elevator ride (for example, thirty seconds and 100-150 words)...

An effective elevator pitch generally answers questions such as:
- What the product is
- What it does for the buyer (e.g. the benefits)
- Who you are"

Basically, an elevator speech is a short introduction to you and your business, carefully crafted with the intent of creating interest from your audience in a very brief period of time. For example, in real estate, an elevator speech might begin something along the lines of "*I help distressed homeowners rediscover finan-*

cial peace." A disability insurance salesperson might say, "*I help people protect their most significant asset—their income.*"

Personally, I'd have trouble keeping a straight face with some scripted elevator speech. As an introvert, I'm hesitant to push myself on anyone without an invitation, and these sorts of statements just feel a bit pushy and scripted to me.

In my experience, both in delivering elevator speeches and being the audience of them, I believe that the most persuasive speech has little to do with the words said, and much more to do with the enthusiasm and excitement in the delivery of those words.

Let me tell you a story to better explain what I mean.

In April of 2006, I began a two-year sabbatical from my real estate career to finish a book I had started three years earlier. Overnight, I went from being a successful real estate agent who owned her own company to being an unemployed, unpublished writer.

In the early days of my sabbatical, I had trouble answering the simple question, "*So, Jennifer, what do you do?*" I was no longer a real estate agent, but neither did I consider myself a writer. After all, I hadn't had anything published and I didn't know if I ever would. So, I'd sort of weasel out of the conversation by almost whispering something like, "*I'm writing a book about real estate.*" Not surprisingly, no one seemed really interested, which was fine with me because I didn't feel comfortable elaborating at that point.

Well, I finished up the book and while it was going through the publishing process, I started selling it as an eBook in the fall of 2006. And started getting really good reviews from my readers. I mean, really good. A few people even said the book changed their lives. Which, as you can imagine, increased my confidence tremendously.

Fast forward a few months.

In January of 2007, I was in a meeting with some nurses and administrators at the nursing home where my mom was living, and we were talking, obviously, about my mom. At the end of the meeting, one of the nurses politely asked me what I did for a living. I found myself sitting up a little straighter and announcing, with a big smile on my face:

"I'm a writer!"

And you wouldn't believe the reaction in the room. Everybody stopped what they were doing, looked at me, and waited to hear more. I started telling them about my book, what it was about, why I wrote it and what I was doing to market it and, I tell ya', I had a captive audience. And believe me, not one of these women had any interest in learning how to be a real estate agent. But two of them asked me for my card so they could tell their agent about me and, as we were leaving, the head administrator told me that I should take my show on the road—**that I was so personable and confident that every real estate agent I met would surely buy my book once they heard me talk about it**.

Huh? Personable? Confident? Those weren't words I could recall being applied to me in recent history, but the administrator was absolutely sincere. A light bulb went off. While, at the time, I'd never heard the term "elevator speech," that's exactly what it turned out to be.

So, how can you use this approach in *your* real estate career?

It's very simple! When someone asks you what you do for a living, smile, throw back your shoulders and say, *"I'm a real estate agent!"* If you say it as if you have the coolest job in the whole world, your audience will be excited with you. And they might just ask for your business card…

The Law of Attraction

No chapter with the term "attract" in the title could fail to mention the now-mainstream concept of the Law of Attraction. If you're one of the few human beings who has not heard of the Law (popularized in the book and 2006 movie "The Secret"), here is the Wikipedia definition:

"According to proponents of this law, thoughts have an energy which attracts whatever it is the person is thinking of. In order to control this energy to one's advantage, proponents state that people must practice four things:

- Know what you want.

- Ask the universe for it.
- Feel and behave as if the object of your desire is on its way.
- Be open to receiving it.

Thinking of what one does not have, they say, manifests itself in not having, while if one abides by these principles, and avoids "negative" thoughts, the universe will manifest a person's desires."

I define it for myself like this: Whatever I focus on, I get more of. If I focus on my worries, I get more to worry about. If I focus on my happiness, I'll get more to be happy about.

There are gobs and gobs of books and articles and videos in which you can learn more about the Law of Attraction, written by philosophers far more educated and eloquent than I.

But to finish off this chapter on attracting business your way, let me share an exercise I've found to be incredibly powerful in my own business-building efforts.

An important part of the Law of Attraction philosophy is the practice of Visualization. To "visualize" means that you close your eyes and imagine your desired outcome playing out, complete with the sights, sounds, smells and feelings associated with it. By the end of your visualizing exercise, you should be literally feeling giddy with excitement—if you can evoke those feelings in yourself, you know you did it right. And gosh darnit if what you visualized about doesn't come to pass more often than not! Give it a try. Once you see it actually work once or twice, you'll feel a sense of power over your life you never imagined you could have.

"It isn't just what you know, and it isn't just who you know. It's actually who you know, who knows you, and what you do for a living."
—Bob Burg, coauthor of
The Go-Giver and Go-Givers Sell More

C H A P T E R   F O U R

Your Sphere of Influence (SOI)

AHHHH…your sphere of influence…the people you know who, if inspired properly, can be the source of most, if not all of your real estate business. Seriously.

No book I might write about real estate would be complete without a thorough discussion* of generating business from one's sphere of influence. If you've spent any time at all in Sell-with-Soul-Land, you already know that I fancy myself a bit of an expert on the topic, although my views, opinions and advice tend to fall somewhat outside the conventional industry views, opinions and advice about the best way to ensure a steady stream of business from the people we know.

But first, a little SOI 101.

What, Exactly, IS a Sphere of Influence Business Model?

A Sphere of Influence business model is a strategy that focuses on attracting business to you from the people you know and the people you meet, as opposed to

---

* In the appendix is a portion of a chapter from my FUN book about sphere of influence business modeling. In the interest of not repeating myself here, I'll direct you there if you aren't already familiar with my sphere of influence philosophies.

pursuing business from strangers. It's possible to run a 100% SOI business and never have to make one cold call, memorize a prospecting script or knock on a stranger's door!

An effective SOI business model has three primary activities.

1. Nurturing the personal relationships you already have within your social network (that is, your friends—I call this group my "Group One." Clever, eh?)
2. Staying in touch with "everyone else" (that is, the people you know who aren't your friends—I call them my Group Two).
3. Meeting new people.

Before you panic and say that you don't have the time, money or energy to do all this socializing, take a deep breath and keep reading!

Running an SOI business is much less time-consuming and less expensive than just about any other systematized prospecting method, and can be far more effective, more quickly. In fact, if you spend a few years creating your personal cheering section, you might be able to pretty much coast through the rest of your real estate career. That's what I did and in my last five years I rarely worked more than 30 hours a week and my marketing budget was practically zero. My phone rang, I answered it, and whaddya' know? I had a new client.

Nurturing the personal relationships you already have

From a philosophical perspective, this means you ensure that the people in your social network (*aka* Group One) know that you care about them. In a practical sense, it means that you strive to have a personal conversation with everyone in your social network as often as you can, at least once a quarter. A personal conversation can be a face-to-face lunch or coffee date, a phone call or even an email exchange. What it's not is a concerted effort to abuse your friends with a sales pitch. Always approach anyone in your social network as a friend first and a real estate agent second, or third, or fourth. Not the other way around.

Staying in touch with Everyone Else

Staying in touch with your "everyone else" group (*aka* Group Two) just means that you keep your name in front of this crowd with periodic interesting, relevant, non-salesy written communications, delivered both through snail-mail and email. As long as your mailings are consistent and intelligent, you'll see a significant number of sales from even this minimal effort.

Meeting new people

An important part of an effective SOI model is to add to your Groups One and Two, especially in today's market where there is admittedly less business to go around. The more people you know, who know you, and think you're a generally cool person, the more that telephone will ring.

Running an effective SOI business model isn't nearly as complicated as some would have you believe. Yes, it takes some organization and commitment upfront, and an ongoing effort to stay in touch with the people you know and the people you meet, but once it's rolling and you're in the SOI habit, it won't feel like work at all! In fact, it might even feel suspiciously like FUN! And "*the more fun you have selling real estate, the more real estate you will sell!*"

The People We Know

This seems as good a place to start as any.

The more I write and talk and think about one's sphere of influence as a source of business, the more I realize that in a real estate career, most, if not all, of one's business ends up at SOI, regardless of where it started.

Here's what I mean.

In the good old days, before the mortgage meltdown and subsequent recession, agents who ran a "sphere of influence" business relied primarily on their social network for leads. They got business directly from the people they knew—when the people they knew hired them and referred them—and indirectly from the social opportunities the people they knew provided to meet new people.

And, in many cases, that was enough. It was for me. Any real estate agent with a decent work ethic and enough sense to stay in touch with the people she knew could depend on those people she knew and the people she met thru the people she knew to provide a steady supply of leads.

During those boom years, it was possible to run a successful, consistent real estate business without venturing much beyond the confines of one's own network of friends and acquaintances. Of course, the more friends and acquaintances an agent had, the more real estate he was likely to sell; that hasn't changed. But in today's more challenging market, where people aren't moving around and investing with abandon the way they did in years past, running a successful sphere of influence business model might require some tweaking of one's definition of sphere of influence!

SOI Redefined for a Post-Meltdown Market

As described in FUN, the best definition of a sphere of influence is: *Everyone who knows you and knows that you sell real estate*. Period. Doesn't matter if the person has ever referred business to you in the past or if you think they'll refer business to you in the future; it doesn't even matter if the person likes you (although it's preferable they do!); if someone knows you and knows that you sell real estate, they are in your sphere of influence.

Traditionally, this definition has been interpreted to include your friends, both close and casual, your family, your acquaintances, your current and past clients and your service providers. And we all know the drill—make a list of these people, enter their contact information into a contact management system, and stay in touch with them forever and ever.

Good plan.

But it occurred to me one day after a conversation with an agent who was resisting the idea of a sphere of influence business model that this definition and approach, while technically accurate, was being misinterpreted and therefore misapplied by real estate agents, even by those who enthusiastically said they embraced the idea of a sphere of influence business model.

This agent I spoke to wasn't comfortable with the idea of pursuing her friends, family and social network for business. Her concerns were typical and understandable. She didn't want to risk her friendships. She didn't think it was appropriate to mix business with pleasure. She didn't want to discount her fees. She didn't wanna, she didn't wanna, she didn't wanna...yada, yada, yada. She categorically stated that she'd much rather work with strangers than with people she already knows.

And that was fine with me. To each his or her own—there are many paths to success in a real estate business and an SOI business model is only one of them. Shoot, there are many paths to success in an SOI business model even!

But I couldn't help myself from arguing just a little with her. Not because I thought I was so smart (*well, maybe...*), but rather because I didn't think she truly understood what an SOI business model can be.

Here's what I shared with her.

Selling real estate to and for your sphere of influence doesn't just mean your friends and acquaintances hire you to be their real estate agent on a consistent-enough basis to keep you in business. It doesn't even mean that they shovel enough referrals your way to keep you in business. Yes, those things will happen, but in today's market, that's not likely to be enough consistent business to keep the dogs fed and those nails polished, especially for an agent in the first few years of her real estate career.

No, a 21st century, post-mortgage-meltdown SOI business model is much broader than simply relying on your friends, family and acquaintances to supply you with leads.

Your sphere of influence is potentially comprised of every living, breathing human being who crosses your path. Of course, not every living breathing human being who crosses your path will become a member of your SOI, but the potential is there. Including those "stranger" leads that the "I don't wanna SOI" crowd is hoping to sell houses to and for.

With me so far?

Even if your business model is based entirely on prospecting to strangers, I have to assume you're hoping that someday you'll meet these strangers, preferably in the context of a real estate transaction. And once you've met them, I have to assume you want to do a great job for them so that they'll tell all their friends about you. And once your transaction with them is over, I assume you'd like to get their future business and referrals, which is best accomplished by staying in touch with them (after you did a great job for them, of course).

So, if these assumptions are true, that sounds pretty much like an SOI business model to me!

Of course, if these assumptions aren't true; if you'd rather continue to pursue strangers for your future business and let anyone you've already met face to face fall by the wayside because they're now a member of your sphere of influence (and you don't wanna SOI), well, okay!

But it seems awfully silly to me.

The truth is, any prospecting strategy that puts you in front of other people can technically be labeled a sphere of influence strategy. To what level you choose to maximize the lead potential of these people you're in front of is up to you, of course. But don't discount the notion of a sphere of influence business model because you don't think it's appropriate to "use" your friendships for business.

But What if…?

But what if you don't know very many people? What if you don't have much of a social network to draw from and, frankly, you're not the type of person who enjoys mingling, networking or broadening your social horizons?

Or what if you truly do feel awkward promoting yourself to the people you do know?

I hear ya! I've been called a functional hermit and I'm usually perfectly happy with my own company! And I've been known to agonize for hours over whether or not my marketing will be welcomed by my target audience…or will simply be an unneeded, unappreciated disruption to their day.

Believe me, you're among friends here.

The Three Branches of Your SOI

First, let's talk about who you know. As we just discussed, every single person you know and every single person you meet is potentially a member of your sphere of influence. Some of them may even become members of your social network.

Um, wait. I must have missed something. Isn't my SOI the same thing as my social network?

Nope. Not at all. And this misunderstanding is a big reason many agents' sphere of influence efforts fail. I talk more about this in FUN (see the Appendix).

Your social network is simply a subset of one of the "branches" of your sphere of influence. There are actually three branches of your sphere of influence.

They are:

1. Your Direct SOI, that is, the people you already know (*aka* Groups one and two)
2. Your Indirect SOI, that is, the people the people you know, know
3. Your Serendipitous SOI, that is, the people you meet as a result of the people you know

Your Direct SOI

These are the people who, today, know you and know you sell real estate, both your "Group One" (your social network) and your "Group Two" (everyone else). These are ALL the people in the world who know you, not just your family and best friends.

You'll get business from your Direct SOI, but it probably won't be your primary source of closings. Why? Simply because most people we know aren't buying or selling houses on a regular basis, even during boom markets.

Your Indirect SOI

These are the people your Direct SOI refers to you. And, of course, once they've been referred to you, they'll become part of your Direct SOI once you've met and you now know each other. Your Indirect SOI should be a fairly consistent source of business for you, assuming the people you know think a lot of you and know how to find you.

Your Serendipitous SOI

These are the people you meet serendipitously as a result of your existing personal relationships. For example, back in my first year in 1996, I met my second and third clients ever at the wedding of a mutual friend. We didn't know each other when we arrived at the wedding, but we met because we both knew the bride. I met another client at a Pridefest parade I attended with some gay friends. Another at a Super Bowl party I was invited to.

Serendipitous: [ser-uhn-dip-i-tuhs] come upon or found by accident; fortuitous

---

Your serendipitous SOI can be an enormous source of business for you, if you're often out there in the world with a smile on your face and your antenna up.

Through your personal relationships with the people you already know, you have the potential to meet their friends and acquaintances, and then to meet THEIR friends and acquaintances and so on. Even if you only know 50 people in the world but all 50 of those people know 50 other people, that's a pool of around 2500 potential clients for you. And of course, every one of those 2500 potential clients knows even more people.

Expanding Your SOI

If, even given the above definitions of your sphere of influence, you still don't feel you know enough people to generate enough business for yourself from the people you know, well, you'll probably want to do something about that. This may seem overwhelming, especially if you're an introvert. I mean, what exactly can you do to "meet people"? I'm with ya there. Meeting people is not something that comes naturally for me.

But since you asked, I'll do my best to answer.

First, make a list of everyone you know. You may be surprised how many people you do know. Keep a notebook with you at all times so you can write down the names of people you think of as you're going about your day.

Set a goal of how many total contacts you want to have by, say, the end of the year. Two hundred is a good number to shoot for. Figure out how many people you need to meet between now and then to reach your goal.

Using a respectful, non-aggressive approach, strive to make new friends. Best friends? No, of course not. Just put up your antenna, put a smile on your face and greet the world like a fresh breath of air. Be sure to treat everyone you meet as someone you might build a relationship with, not just as someone who might someday become a customer. (But remembering that they could become a customer someday might motivate you to be friendlier than you're otherwise inclined to be.)

We talk more about how to painlessly meet people to add to your sphere of influence in the next chapter.

"I Don't Want to Annoy Anyone!"

Now let's hit your hesitation to market yourself to the people you know, in fear of irritating, annoying, bothering or otherwise making them frown.

BRAVO! Clap clap clap clap!

I love that you're hesitating just a little bit, worrying how your friends will feel about your attempts to prospect to them. That's exactly the right attitude to have when it comes to your precious sphere of influence! Don't ever let anyone tell you that you shouldn't worry about it, that you should just shovel out your marketing without any consideration for the effect it will have on your audience.

Because, believe me, the people you know are not sitting at home, waiting anxiously to be marketed to by you. And you know that, deep inside.

So rest easy. Nothing I'll tell you will put your friendships at risk. I promise.

Keep reading.

The Best Way to Ask for Business (Don't)

No book about prospecting would be complete without a thorough discussion of the value of begging-for-business. Oops, did I say that out loud? I mean, the value of reminding everyone you know and everyone you meet that Referrals are the Lifeblood of Your Business and how The Greatest Compliment You Can Pay Me is the Referral of Your Friends and Family or, just simply, how much You <INSERT BIG RED HEART> Referrals! Ooooh, just makes you feel all warm and fuzzy, doesn't it?

In a word…BLECH.

Lest you wonder where I stand on the issue of asking for business and referrals, let me state it right here, right now, right in your face.

Asking for business and referrals tells your friends that you are desperate for business. That you aren't as successful as you'd like to be. That you haven't been able to build a business based on your reputation and accolades of your satisfied past clients.

Are these things true? Maybe. In fact, probably!

All of us started somewhere and we've all had days, weeks, months or even years when we ARE feeling desperate for business, when we AREN'T as successful as we'd like to be and when we AREN'T seeing the repeat and referral business we feel we deserve. That's the nature of how we make our living; and even the most successful agents had or even still have periods where they feel vulnerable and uncertain.

But why, oh why do we real estate agents feel the need to advertise this fact? Oh, sure, sometimes you just can't help it—when you're commiserating with a friend or participating in a gripe session with other agents or crying to your spouse—it can be hard to keep a smile on your face. It's awfully tempting, sometimes uncontrollably so, to vent your discouragement to anyone who will listen.

But that doesn't mean that it's okay to purposely share this emotion with your prospects!

I'll Be Happy to Refer to You as Long as It's My Idea...(that is, please don't ask me to)

I got a facial the other day. Some fancy schmantzy European Spa Facial with a massage. Yummy. It was really good. And, I swear, I look ten years younger.

So, I'm lying there trying to enjoy being cleansed, exfoliated, moisturized and massaged. Yet, I'm tense. I'm waiting for the...facial-ist(?)...to ask me if I'd be willing to send her referrals.

Seriously, I could hardly relax preparing myself for the inevitable sales pitch.

I pondered this behind my moisturizing mask. Why was I so opposed to her asking me for referrals? Not because I wouldn't refer her—she was definitely refer-worthy, and I was actually kind of excited about handing out her business card to my friends.

But I wanted to refer her on my own terms, not because she asked me to! I wanted to surprise her with my referrals. I like thinking that this wonderful facial-ist doesn't desperately need my referrals, but that she would certainly appreciate them, as one professional to another.

This story has a happy ending—she did not try to sell me anything—not an expensive cleanser or moisturizer or serum; nor did she beg me for my future business or referrals. And...I grabbed a handful of her cards on the way out!

Okay, now that that's out of my system, let's back up a bit. Why am I so opposed to asking for business when every other sales trainer on the planet swears it's your duty to do so?

Why Is It Wrong to Ask for Business?

Oh, let me count the reasons…

- **First, asking for business is unnecessary**. If you do a good job for me, I'm your biggest fan. I'm delighted to hand out your card or point people to your website if I'm impressed with you. You sure don't have to ask me to; in fact, I'd much prefer that you didn't. Aren't you the same way?

  When someone knocks your sox off with their service, don't you happily return to them and refer them to others when the opportunity arises? Sure you do! And chances are you weren't asked to do so; it just came naturally to you. We all like to be a resource for our friends; it makes us appear smart to be able to have an answer to the question "*Hey, do you know anyone good who…?*" with confidence. And ooooh, even smarter when our referral goes well!

- **Second, asking for business and referrals can be counterproductive to your goal of actually getting business and referrals**. Think about your own hiring and referral patterns. Do you hire people you feel sorry for…or people you know will take excellent care of you or your friend? The latter, of course.

  You don't hire someone because you know they need the business; you hire them because they'll do a good job. And when we refer, we want to feel that the referrals we give are to successful and competent people because referring can be risky business if the referral goes bad. When someone always seems to be on the hunt for business, it may be perceived by the people he knows as desperation or, at the very least, just a little annoying.

- **Third, asking for business puts the other person on the spot**. Sorry, but I get real irritated with my friends when they ask me for business and referrals. If I want to send them business, I'll do it, but if I don't, there may be a reason. As I said above, I can be someone's biggest fan, but my enthusiasm is considerably dampened when my friend puts me on the spot and implies an obligation on my part to send business to her. Yep, I'm rebellious enough to withhold my precious business when someone makes me feel obligated to them. So there!

- **Fourth, asking for business and referrals is unprofessional**. I have the world's greatest accountant. I've used him for years and have sent him tons of referrals. He's expensive, but worth it. However, several years ago he left a long-term partnership and opened his own accounting firm. In conjunction with his venture, he sent out a mass-mailed letter to his current clients thanking us for our continued support and then specifically asking for referrals. Even though this happened long before I'd given any thought to the concept of begging-for-business, I distinctly recall being taken aback by the letter.

  My accountant was so good that I figured he had plenty of business—and I had actually felt a little honored to be his client. But once he made the simple request that I send him referrals, the level of admiration and respect I felt for him slipped a notch. Suddenly he went from being a trusted advisor with a long waiting list to…a run-of-the-mill almost-salesperson who needed my help building his business. Hmmmmm.

  Now, to his credit, he's never repeated this begging-for-business effort and I still happily send referrals to him. But I hope you see how just this one referral-begging campaign tarnished my opinion of his profession-alism and exclusivity.

But if You Don't Ask, You Won't Get!

Agents love to argue with me about my stance on referral-begging. They say: "*If you don't ask, you don't get*" in relation to calling up their spheres of influence (or even strangers) and asking if they know anyone to refer to them.

Of course it's true that in many situations, you must ask for what you want to have any chance of getting what you want. If you would like an unadvertised discount on a computer at Best Buy, you'll have to ask for one. If you'd like fries with your Big Mac, you'll have to ask for them. If you'd like a nicer office, you'll probably have to ask for it.

But when it comes to inspiring people to send business your way—it's a whole 'nother thing. You're "asking" people to think highly enough of you to entrust their precious referral business to you—and as we all know, referrals can backfire on the referrer if they don't go well. Therefore, it's important that you exude an air of success and confidence, which does NOT involve asking/begging/bribing or obligating for business.

Blah Blah Blah—if you've been around here any time at all, you already know how I feel about asking for business. Don't.

But here's the thing. You absolutely can inspire the people you know and the people you meet to send business your way without ever asking/begging/bribing or obligating them to.

How?

Referral-Begging 101

Well, let's go back to Referral-Begging 101. We're taught a variety of scripts to help us Beg for Referrals from our spheres of influence. How about these gems?

- "Do you know anyone who needs to buy or sell real estate?"
- "Do you know anyone moving to my area who could use my services?"
- "I build my business by referral; will you please keep me in mind if you hear of anyone buying or selling?"
- "I'm never too busy for your referrals."
- "I'm always looking for referrals, so would you mind taking a few of my business cards?"

So, Jennifer, um, I don't get it. What's wrong with these scripts?

Say each of them out loud. What message are your words sending to your audience?

Did you notice how all these scripts are all about YOU (as in, the person saying the scripts)? All about what YOU need and want?

There's nothing in these scripts that leads your audience to believe you have anything of value for them; you aren't assuring them of your competence, of your expertise, of your work ethic. You aren't telling them with your words or tone or even your body language that you **are capable** of Taking Great Care of Them and Their Referrals. No, you're simply telling them with your words, your tone and your body language that you **need** Their Business and Referrals.

And in case you didn't catch it the first or second or third time I said it…people don't hire and refer out of pity; they hire and refer to people they think will do a great job.

So, how could you let the people you know and the people you meet know that you'll "take great care of their business" as opposed to you just "need their business"?

And, no, the answer probably isn't telling them, "I'll take great care of your business, I promise!"

The answer is fairly simple, but it involves shifting your paradigm FROM marketing yourself from an "*I need business*" perspective TO an "*I'd be delighted to help you (and I'm perfectly capable of doing so)*" one. It's not a script or a dialogue; it's an internal conviction.

Keep reading. By the end of the book, I think you'll have your answer.

Taking Begging-for-Business to the Next Level—Bribing for Business!

Here's another topic near and dear to my heart. Bribery.

Don't do it.

Well, duh, you say.

But it's possible you've already done it. Have you ever offered special deals, juicy referral bonuses or gifts, or contributions to the charity-of-choice in exchange for business or referrals? Have you tried to encourage people to hire and refer you, not based on your exceptional service but on your exceptional kick-backs?

Most of us have tried this approach; I have, more than once. But has it worked? I'll bet it hasn't. Sure, there are those who have taken advantage of our generous offers, but they'd have hired or referred us anyway, probably. I doubt we got any extra business from our bribery efforts. And we took an enormous, unnecessary risk.

Oh, I know our heart's in the right place. We have only good intentions by offering rebates, gifts and referral fees, but it will backfire. The people we know will be happy to send business our way if they think we'll take good care of it. Offering an "incentive" makes us look desperate and somewhat unprofessional.

This is not to say that you shouldn't thank someone for sending business your way, oh, no! In fact, it would be terribly rude not to! But y'know what? A sincere Thank You will go just as far as an expensive gift when showing your appreciation. Maybe even further. People just want to be acknowledged and appreciated and besides, the best way to reward referral behavior is to make the referrer proud of his referral. That means...take great care of that referred client!

Obligation

Once we get past begging and bribing, we get to the absolutely worst method of generating business and referrals for ourselves.

Implying (or even demanding) obligation from your sphere of influence.

A few years ago I participated in a lively online discussion about how a new real estate agent was heartbroken (and subsequently outraged) that his brother-in-law hired someone else to sell his home. Because he was brand new, he felt his B.I.L. owed it to him to give him the listing so that he'd get some much-needed experience. The new agent was bad-mouthing his B.I.L. to the rest of the family and swearing to avoid him at the next family get-together.

OUCH!

How fast can you say, "Kiss Your Family's Business Goodbye?"

No one on this planet is obligated to work with us, regardless of any personal relationship. Instead of whining and sulking and pouting about the situation, our new agent should have taken all that energy and asked himself why his brother-in-law didn't hire him. And made an effort to do better next time.

Was it personal? Maybe, maybe not. Although, with this guy's attitude, it probably was. The minute I get a sense that someone feels I'm obligated to hire or refer them, I'm turned off. Yeah, I'm contrary that way, aren't you?

Getting business from the people you know is an art that, once mastered, will seem oh-so-obvious and natural. But if you approach the people you know with the attitude that they owe you something because you're related or went to college together or because you sent them a pretty calendar last year, your prospecting efforts with them will crash and burn.

What I would have advised the new agent to do (had he asked) would be to graciously accept defeat and cheerfully offer his assistance. I'd have told him to be pleasant, supportive and complimentary of the other agent's efforts. Sweet as sugar. Because...at some point, the B.I.L might just get frustrated with the agent he selected and be open to talking again.

But instead, look what this guy did. He alienated his B.I.L. and gave the entire family a great reason to wonder about his professionalism. I'll bet that it will be a long time before anyone in that family dares to talk to him about their own real estate needs!

I know that when you're a real estate agent, you really do crave the support of the people you know and, yes, it will sting when you find out that a friend or family member "cheated" on you. When it happens, you have my permission to sulk, pout or even cry into your pillow that night. But do your sulking, pouting and crying in the privacy of your own home and never, ever take those emotions out into the world with you. There's absolutely no benefit and oh, my, all sorts of harm that can come of it.

But, But, But…!

All rightee, let's deal with your objections!

OBJECTION #1—There's no harm in asking, right?

I believe differently. I believe there are all kinds of harm in asking for business. And no, asking for what you want is not always the most efficient route to getting what you want. Ever heard of playing hard to get? Or reverse psychology?

Imagine if you were to interrogate a typical guy about his plans for your future together on your first (or tenth) date…he'll likely run for the hills regardless of his feelings on the matter. Or if you repeatedly beg your friends to play match-maker, they may silently wonder why you're so desperate, and be unwilling to subject their USDA Prime Choice male friends to that desperation (after all, matchmaking often backfires on the matchmaker!).

OBJECTION #2—If I don't ask my friends for business, how will they know I want it?

The short answer is that…they just will.

The longer answer is that as long as your friends think you're a reasonably competent human being, and they know what you do for a living AND they know where to find your phone number—AND they've heard from you recently, you have a great shot at being the agent of choice in their world. This means that you'll get their business, you'll probably get their family's business and your name will be mentioned if their friends ever have a need for someone like you. Once your name gets around in a few social circles, you'll see business naturally start to come in.

"Dear SOI, I Don't Want Your 'Loyalty'"

One of my readers asked the question, "How do you build loyalty with your customers or potential customers?"

Interesting question.

I don't. I don't want anyone's "loyalty." Oh, sure I'll take it, but to me, the word "loyalty" is on the same playing field as "obligation," which as I've said before is a Dirty Word When You SOI. I don't want anyone to feel obligated to be loyal to me!

I want to earn my business, and keep earning it. I want my customers to use me, hire me and refer me…then use me, hire me and refer me again…and again…not because they're "loyal," but because they know I'm good at my job, they like me and they know I care deeply about their real estate transaction.

So, how do I make sure they know this?

By being a darn good real estate agent (which means I know my market, my systems and my contracts, among other things), by staying in touch with the people I know… and by never pestering them about being loyal!

But a lot of agents are concerned, reasonably so, that their friends don't know how they work—that they DO want and need business and that if they don't let their friends know this, they'll innocently hire or refer someone else.

Quite true. But there are better ways of letting people know how you work without putting them on the spot. For example, when you have social conversations with the people you know, you can casually mention a referral you just received that you're excited about. Or, when talking with a prospect, try this phrase, "I love working by referral because I meet the nicest people!" which not only gets the point across that you do work by referral, but also implies that you think your prospect is one of those "nicest people"!

In reality, if you're good at what you do and you love what you do, that will be apparent to the people in your world and they'll want to support you. Conversely, if you take the approach of begging for business, that sends the opposite message.

OBJECTION #3—I'm afraid that if I don't ask my friends for business, they'll think I'm too busy.

The only way your friends will think you're too busy for them is if you act as if you're too busy. If you don't return phone calls, show up late, always appear rushed and frazzled, or drop the ball on social engagements...then yes, the people you know may hesitate to send you business.

But there's a big difference between being successfully busy and "too" busy. Have you ever noticed that when you're crazy-busy, more business seems to pour in? People want to work with those who are successful.

OBJECTION #4—I'd rather take the risk of annoying my friends rather than take the risk of losing a referral.

I understand...but I disagree. When you systematically ask for business, you are very likely to annoy your friends and that's a risk you should never take.

I got an email once from a client asking permission to give my name to two friends who were looking for a real estate agent. Asking my permission! Just in case I might be too busy to handle even more clients. And you know what? This is exactly the impression I want to leave with my world.

By not overtly letting my client know that I <Heart> Referrals, I took the chance that she wouldn't know to send me any. I took the chance, that, egads, she might send her friends to someone else! Oh the horror!!

However, I'd much rather take the chance of losing potential referrals out of innocent ignorance than to take the chance of annoying, pestering or otherwise damaging my credibility with my SOI by constantly reminding them to send business my way.

In fact, I'd rather risk being forgotten all together than risk being annoying!

I know that if I do a great job for my clients and treat them respectfully, they will think of me when the topic of real estate comes up in their social interactions. If they don't think of me, well, it won't have anything to do with whether I pestered them lately about it...but everything to do with their respect for me as a professional real estate agent.

OBJECTION #5: I've always asked for business and it's always worked for me.

Fair enough. You are an adult human being and I trust your judgment. However, allow me to offer a few thoughts to ponder.

First, it's possible that you are among the very few who are actually skilled at asking for business. Every once in a while, I'll run into someone who somehow manages to inspire me with their business-begging to actually want to hire or refer them. (When that happens, I should take better notes!) But it's rare and the vast majority of the time, any attempt at business-begging irritates me. If you believe with all your heart that you are among this minority, then you have my blessing to continue what you're doing.

Second, I'll bet $100 that you'd get most of that business anyway, even if you didn't ask/beg/bribe for it. You're good at what you do and your clientele likes you; that's obvious because, if they didn't, they wouldn't refer you no matter what you did or said. In fact, I'll go out on a limb and say that you might enjoy an even more robust referral-based business if you didn't impose your business-begging on your clientele because they'd feel less obligated to do it. Obligation does NOT equal affection, unfortunately.

Third, I wonder if you don't lose a little repeat business from customers who don't like being put on the spot. If I knew that every time (or even every third time) I visited my massage therapist she was going to sweetly ask me for referrals, I promise you I'd find a new massage therapist.

Seven Alternatives to Begging/Bribing/Obligating for Business

So, let's say I've convinced you that Begging/Bribing/Obligating is wrong and you promise never to do it again. Cool. So what should you do instead?

Well, first, it's sort of a misnomer to call this section "Alternatives" to referral-begging. Why? Because, unless begging for referrals is your sole prospecting strategy, there really isn't an "alternative" approach. **Just don't do it.** Do whatever it is you do to generate business for yourself and leave the referral-begging/bribing/obligating out of it.

But what DO you do instead? How can you let your friends and family and acquaintances and clients know that you'd really love their business and referrals, without looking desperate?

It's really not hard to let people know in a non-threatening way that you enjoy a referral-based business. See how I worded that? That you "**enjoy a referral-based business.**" That sounds a whole lot more professional than any of the "I ♥ Referrals!" or "Oh, by the way...Do you know anyone...?" or "The Greatest Compliment I Receive is...," doesn't it? Kind of like it just happens naturally, without effort...cause you're so Darn COOL!" Which you are, aren't you?

Here are seven casual ways to do that (without a hint of begging, bribing or obligating):

1. Tell an interesting story about a referral you received.

2. Tell a story about an interesting new client you got who wasn't a referral

(which surprised you since "almost all your business comes from referrals.")

3. Casually mention that you love working by referral because you get to meet such nice people (like you, my dear new client).

4. If you get a client from traditional prospecting, express your surprise that he or she found you since (again) "most of your business comes from referrals."

5. Assume you'll receive referrals from friends and clients by casually saying something like, "If you send a referral my way, be sure to give them my website so they can check me out ahead of time!"

6. If you feel you must make a statement about referrals on your business card, blog or other marketing material, convey a sentiment of confidence, not desperation, such as "Referrals Happily Accepted" or "Referrals Welcome."

7. If someone asks you about your real estate business, see if you can slip in the phrase, "Well, since I work mostly by referral…" ("I don't advertise," "I can focus more attention on my clients," "My family life isn't nearly as affected as it is for those who are always prospecting for new business," etc.).

Are You an RCHB?

One of my favorite concepts to talk about in relation to a sphere of influence business model is that of the "RCHB." RCHB stands for a "Reasonably Competent Human Being." When you come across as an RCHB to other people, they are much more likely to consider honoring you with their real estate business than they will be if you come across as, um, flaky.

The good news is that being an RCHB is pretty easy to demonstrate to people you know and people you meet, whether you're meeting them as a real estate agent or just as a friend or new acquaintance. The bad news is that it's also very easy to come across as a Non-RCHB (*aka*, a flake). Coming across as a flake to the people you know and the people you meet will be deadly to your prospecting efforts, even if those people like you on a personal level.

This is even more important for new or newer agents without a database of Satisfied Past Clients to rely on—by definition, all of your business is going to come from people who haven't yet tried you out and must make the decision to hire you based on the impression they have of you.

So, if you're going to rely on your sphere of influence for business, you may have to watch yourself a little closer to ensure that you're presenting yourself as a competent, positive, reliable, trustworthy, ethical type of guy or gal. Please don't take this as an implied criticism of YOUR trustworthiness or reliability—even I have to keep an eye on myself when I'm socializing to ensure that I'm not venting too much or telling stories that make me appear flaky or careless or sometimes, even, not quite above-board.

Anyway, more good news for new real estate agents is that if you come across as an RCHB to your friends and acquaintances, most won't be too concerned about your lack of experience selling real estate. The general public doesn't think our job is very hard, so if you appear to be reliable, intelligent and ethical, in many cases, that will be enough to make someone consider hiring you.

***

Okay, fine. RCHB it is. But, um, Jennifer, what specifically can I do to demonstrate to the people I know and the people I meet that I am an RCHB?

Glad you asked! I've come up with six characteristics of a Reasonably Competent Human Being—all of which are 100% within your control.

Do You Refer to Your Flaky Friends?
(Or, egads, are you the flaky one?)

My friends are mostly self-employed. Real estate agents, yes, but also lenders, insurance agents, dog-trainers, chiropractors, massage therapists and home stagers, all of whom, like me, would greatly appreciate the good will (i.e., business and referrals) of their friends (i.e., their spheres of influence).

But I tell ya...some of the self-employed folks in my social circle are...well...socially flaky. They don't return phone calls quickly, if at all. They cancel our lunch date at the last minute, or show up 30 minutes late (without a phone call). They promise to look into something for me and never do. They throw around four-letter words like a drunken college kid. They borrow a book and never return it. They RSVP to my dinner party and don't show up.

And then...they beg me for referrals.

Sorry, but I just can't do it. I love my friends, but if they aren't reliable in my personal interactions with them, I can't take the chance that they'll treat my precious referral business any better.

Oh, I'll admit, I'm not perfect in my social life, either. If I'm crazy busy, my clients come first and I will cancel on a friend. I've also been known to let my introversion get the best of me and not show up to a wedding, funeral or housewarming party I'm expected to be at. But I realize when I do that I may very well be damaging a potentially lucrative professional relationship, so I really really, really try to hold up my end of the social bargain.

In our business, you can never truly separate business from pleasure, unless you truly don't want business and referrals from your social network. And that would be kinda crazy, wouldn't it?

An RCHB...

- Is almost always on time
- Returns phone calls promptly
- Strives for 100% error-free written material
- Watches her language
- Is emotionally mature
- Does what she says she's going to do

- *Item 1: Be on Time* is self-explanatory. Don't be late. Not for business appointments, social engagements or your massage. Remember, every single person you come in contact with has the potential to be your biggest fan. Don't blow it by disrespecting their precious time or looking too unorganized or flustered to show up when promised.

    I realize that some human beings simply don't have the Be-On-Time gene and are always always always late. It's simply part of who they are and, contrary to what most of us always-on-timers believe, I don't think it's a sign that the always-late person is disrespectful or doesn't care about us or our busy schedules. However, notice what I just said—the perception that the always-late are disrespectful or uncaring is pretty prevalent in society and you aren't going to change that perception. On a social level, your friends might put up with your always-late-ness, but it will definitely put doubt in their minds that you're an RCHB. And it will most certainly hurt your chances with potential clients.

- *Item 2: Return phone calls promptly*. Return all calls as soon as you can, **not just business ones**. You only have a short window to return a phone call promptly. If you wait five hours or even overnight, you've blown it. Sure, you can apologize or offer excuses, but that won't even come close to the positive impression you'll make on someone if you return their call in five minutes.

    My first year as a real estate agent, I carried a pager (this was back when cell phone minutes were very expensive, so often we kept our numbers a secret!) and returned calls as soon as I was paged. I can't tell you how often I got a new client because I was the first person to return a phone call.

Some worry that by returning phone calls too quickly they'll come across as desperate, but I'd rather you take that chance rather than the reverse—that the person doesn't think you care about them or wonders if you're organized enough to take care of their needs.

Recently I called a mortgage broker on a Friday morning and she didn't return my call until Monday afternoon. She apologized, saying her computer had crashed and she'd spent all weekend working on it—understandable—but it didn't erase the perception that she didn't care about my business or, again, was too unorganized to take care of me.

I heard some advice recently on this topic—it's from the olden days before cell phones and cordless phones—but it was that after you listen to a message on your voicemail, don't even put the phone back on the cradle. Just clear the line and make the return phone call. Even if you don't have an answer yet.

- ***Item 3: Strive for 100% error-free written material.*** Obviously, this applies to any promotional material you create (personal brochures, newsletters, website, etc.) but also any personal communication between you and your SOI.

  Your announcement or reconnection letter and even your emails should be pretty darn clean. Not everyone is a terrific speller or grammar-phile, but please make the effort. I'd hate to see you chase off even one referral because you can't find the spell-check button or figure out how to capitalize the first word in a sentence.

  There's an agent on an online forum I participate in who continually apologizes for his sloppy posts with the implied message that he's just too busy to do it right. Which comes across that it's not important to him to do it right and he doesn't care about his audience. He actually has a lot of intelligent commentary, but it's lost in the difficult-to-read manner in which he posts.

Again, apologizing or rationalizing is a poor substitute for just doing it right.

- **Item 4: *Watch your language*.** I hope the following doesn't offend you. If you want to demonstrate your professionalism to the people you know, you need to cut down on the four-letter words. It's a habit many of us have, but unfortunately is a habit that can cost us business. I have a friend who is an insurance agent, but her language is so rough I wouldn't dream of referring anyone to her. I'm sure she wonders why. Does she behave that way with her clients? I don't know, but I'm not willing to take the chance with my precious referral business.

I have a tough time with this one and it's a constant struggle for me. I love four-letter words and I think it's fun to toss them around because I don't look like someone who talks like that. But when I make a concerted effort to watch my language, I'm stunned at how noticeable it is when others curse around me and how jarring it is to my psyche. If you're like me and have trouble with this concept—take a one week break from using any bad words and see if you become more sensitized to others' use of them.

An agent friend of mine agonized for hours over whether or not to tell a mortgage broker she'd recently met why she didn't intend to refer buyers to him. We discussed it and decided that it would be her good deed of the day to be honest with him. What was her hesitation? He freely threw the f-bomb around in their conversations and, even though she's been known to toss her own bombs around from time to time, she didn't feel she knew him well enough for him to feel comfortable speaking to her in that manner. Therefore, she was worried he'd take similar liberties with her clients.

His response to her well-intentioned advice to tone down the language? Defensiveness, mostly, which is understandable. He explained that he spoke that way with her because he did feel comfortable with her and further, wanted to "prove" his personal comfort by speaking in a manner that was clearly inappropriate among strangers. And I get that. I've done it, too. But this little anecdote drove it home (again) for me that it's not worth the risk of offending someone!

Something related to this is that you need to watch how you talk about your vices. Let me tell you a personal story. When I was in my early 30's, my husband and I were wine snobs. We drank a bottle of wine every night, sometimes followed by a glass or two of port or Baileys or some other yummy dessert drink. All our friends were the same way—we were a crowd of yuppie winos, frankly. All our social activities involved alcohol and we were often tipsy by 7p.m.

When my husband and I divorced, I stopped drinking for a while—not with a concerted effort, but just because my lifestyle changed. And once I was away from it, I was stunned at how much my friends talked about alcohol. It was jarring to me to realize how central alcohol was in our lives and disconcerting to realize that I used to talk the same way, even to my clients I didn't socialize with. I came to discover, much to my surprise, that not everyone in the world comes home and opens a bottle of wine every night and it was probably very off-putting for me to conversationally share that part of my life with people who did not share the lifestyle.

A more dramatic example is a girlfriend of mine who has smoked pot most of her adult life. To her, smoking pot is a natural thing to do and she seems to assume that everyone does it. She often makes comments in mixed company about being high or stoned, without apology, as if her audience can relate. Of course, some can, but many, myself included, can't.

If you have friends who have seen you drunk or high or in other compromising situations, you may have trouble convincing them that you're an RCHB, especially if you're still partaking in these activities with them.

I'm not the moral police—far from it—but just know that these people may never be good sources of business for you.

- ***Item 5: Be emotionally mature.*** Huh? This is another potentially touchy subject. And, females, it's mostly directed at us. Some of our friends have seen us at our most pathetic, haven't they? And we've seen them at theirs. But, as someone who is hoping to project a professional persona to her friends, you might have to tone that down, or at least be very particular to whom you...um..."talk" to. It may be difficult for your sob-sister to see you as a competent professional. I've had a few girlfriends in my life whose personal lives were such a mess I truly couldn't imagine they could perform professionally in a work environment. I'm sure they did, but, as much as I loved them, I simply wasn't confident in their professional abilities.

  Unfortunately, being emotionally mature can even apply at home. Do you come home and whine to your spouse about your business or your clients or the market? Or do you express your confidence and optimism? This is a call you'll have to make, but do realize that your spouse may question your competence if you seem to always be distressed about your job. It can be difficult for our families, including a spouse, to make a referral to us because if the referral goes bad, it will reflect negatively on the person doing the referring. So, like it or not, you'll need to worry about this RCHB business even in the safety and comfort of your home.

- ***Item 6: Do what you say you're going to do.*** Strive to never let anyone down. Don't cancel at the last minute or simply not show up. Learn to love a to-do list if you don't already. If you tell someone you'll call, call. If you RSVP to a party, go. If you promise to put a check in the mail, do it NOW! If you owe someone money, pay it promptly. If you borrow a book, return it in a reasonable amount of time.

  Again, apologies don't overcome bad behavior, no matter how compelling your excuse. Just do the right thing instead of trying to come up with a convincing reason you didn't.

***

Notice that none of these six items have much to do with being a good real estate agent. That's because if a friend or acquaintance has never used you as a real estate agent, there's no way to prove to them that you're a good one until they do. And, of course, it's not effective to simply tell someone what a great real estate agent you are—you have to show them, which you can't do until they hire you. But if you come across as a generally reliable, responsive, intelligent, competent person, most people will assume that you're a good real estate agent, too.

Don't Apologize...Just Do It Right!

Do you ever do this...apologize, or even make excuses for something you SHOULD have done right...but it was kind of inconvenient, so you came up with an explanation? For example...you run out of toner in your printer while creating a CMA for a seller prospect...so you apologize for not bringing the CMA with you to your listing appointment? Or you're feeling fat, so you wear your overalls to a coffee date and apologize for how you look? Or you don't feel like washing your car...so you apologize to your new buyer for the condition of your automobile?

I've done all three of these in the last week alone. In fact, as I write this, I'm sitting at my computer in my overalls (okay, so they're designer overalls, but still) trying to work up the energy to change* before a dinner date with my friend Lezlie.

There are all kinds of opportunities in this world to mess up or otherwise demonstrate to the people you know and the people you meet that you aren't on top of your game. These opportunities present themselves on a pretty regular basis, often without warning, so I'm thinking that anytime I can actually control a potentially credibility-killing situation, I should take advantage of it.

When I run out of toner...I should buck up and go pay $35 for a replacement cartridge at Office Max (as opposed to $3.84 at my favorite online toner store www.inkamerica. com). Similarly, if I run out of nice paper in the middle of preparing said CMA, I really should take that 20 minutes and go buy some more. And how long does it take to run your car through a car wash and vacuum out the inside?

We've all heard how You Only Have One Chance to Make a First Impression. Don't let a little laziness (or feeling fatness) damage your next opportunity to make a great one...

* Nope, I didn't change. My laziness got the better of me...

One day in mid-2010, three different people suggested I read *The Go-Giver* by Bob Burg and John David Mann. It wasn't the first time I'd heard that, but on this particular day, I heard it three times.

I took it as a sign, fired up the Kindle and forked over the $18.99 for immediate upload to my digital reader. Since I was traveling, I was able to dive right in to find out what all the fuss was about.

Wow.

These guys have been stealing my stuff. Or, maybe I've been stealing theirs. Or maybe (*she says modestly*) Great Minds Just Think Alike. But for those who have suggested I write a *Sell with Soul* for the general public; well, it's already been done by Mr. Burg and Mr. Mann. Exceptionally well, I might add, and (not without a trace of envy), a wee bit more successfully!

If you haven't read *The Go-Giver*, or the sequel, *Go-Givers Sell More*…well, do! But in case you haven't yet had the pleasure, the basic premise of the Go-Giver philosophy is that, in order to be successful in a sales career (or any career, really, or truthfully, in life itself!), you'll be far better off putting other people's needs, wants and desires ahead of your own. Not just because it's the polite thing to do (that good ol' Golden Rule and all), but because it's simply a smart way to live and love. And yes, succeed.

The authors, Mr. Mann and Mr. Burg, focus primarily on salespeople perhaps because traditional sales training and wisdom teaches its practitioners just the opposite—what one might call a Go-TAKER philosophy. That it's all about the salesperson—her wants, needs and desires—and how she can best convince her target/prospect/victim that he wants what she, the salesperson, wants him to want!

(Whew, that was a mouthful).

But Misters Mann and Burg turn that paradigm on its head. They insist (brilliantly and persuasively) that when you make your approach all about the other person, when you truly and sincerely put their needs, wants and desires above your own, you're pretty darned likely to come out ahead. Not ahead of the other person, mind you, but ahead of where you'd be if you'd made it all about you.

Here's the thing. When you sell for a living (and for the sake of simplicity, let's consider real estate a sales career for a few minutes even though I'm of the strong opinion it's not), you are dependent on the good will, trust and support of other people who inhabit the planet with you. You can't be a successful salesperson all by yourself; you need customers, who are in all likelihood going to be human beings. ☺

Therefore, it only makes sense that you might want to behave in ways that will make those other human beings like and trust you—which is best accomplished, not with aggressive sales pitches, but by treating them the way they want to be treated.

In other words, *"It's not about you, it's about them."*

So, how can we apply Go-Giver principles to a real estate business? Oh, my, the applications are practically endless! All you have to do is peruse the typical real estate franchise training manual or read the typical real estate guru book or attend a typical turn-your-business-around-with-my-system live event and you'll find plenty of ideas for doing things in a Go-Giver fashion—**by doing exactly the opposite of what you hear or read there!**

Unfortunately, our industry is obsessed with self-protection and looking out for the ME above all others. And our training reflects that.

> We're encouraged to assault others with a sales pitch they'd rather not be assaulted by because at the end of the day, the end justifies the means if we get a client…
> … instead of creating a message and delivery that will be welcomed by others.
> We're cautioned against giving potential buyers more than a few minutes of our time if they balk at committing to an exclusive arrangement…
> … instead of taking the time to prove ourselves deserving of their commitment.
> We're trained to snottily rebuff a seller's (reasonable) request that we justify our (hefty) fee…

... instead of providing a clear, coherent and persuasive explanation of our commission structure.

We are taught that the best way to approach a For Sale by Owner (FSBO) is with an arsenal of intelligence-insulting material intended to make him feel stupid...

... instead of approaching him with a sincere desire to help.

We're assured that repeatedly pestering our friends for business is perfectly acceptable behavior...

...instead of inspiring our friends to refer to us because we're the best real estate agent they know.

We're taught to trick people into giving us their contact information at open houses...

...instead of inspiring them to want us to have it.

We search for ways to push buyers off the fence...

... instead of helping them decide if now is the right time, for them, to buy a home.

We memorize closing scripts to persuade sellers to sign on the line that is dotted...

...instead of helping them determine if selling makes sense, for them, right now, in today's market and given their personal situation.

I could probably fill up several chapters; maybe even a whole book telling you why I like the Go-Giver philosophy so much, but that would be silly! You don't need me to decide such things for you—read the book yourself and see what you think.

Seriously, it's good stuff. Career-changing stuff. Which makes it life-changing stuff...

"If you smile at someone, they might smile back."
—Author Unknown

CHAPTER FIVE

Be Pleasant to Ten People a Day

WHEN you saw the title to this chapter, what did you think? Did you wonder why on earth anyone would need to advise you to Be Pleasant to people? Or conversely, did you worry about how on earth you would find the time (or get up the nerve) to Be Pleasant to people?

Either way, I believe this simple concept might just be the most paradigm-shifting one in the entire Prospecting with Soul philosophy. By that, I mean it might completely change the way you interact with the world on a daily basis... and you know what? Your future clients are out there in that world, looking for someone just like you.

Your future clients aren't all visiting open houses or wandering into your office or surfing your website or blog. Some of them are, but most, nope—they're at the coffee shop, at Walmart, at the mall, at the dog park, at the Jiffy Lube, at the high school football game, at the PTA meeting, at your spouse's office... they're everywhere you are, which is one of the beautiful things about a real estate career. Our potential clients aren't all in one club or industry or location—they're everywhere.

A few months ago, I had a conversation with an agent who had recently read *Sell with Soul* and was looking for some additional guidance. As we were talking about prospecting and business-building, she complimented me on my anti-pushy salesperson philosophy. She explained that she herself hates to be pushed, and appreciated my advice not to do unto others that which you don't want done unto you.

Okay, that's cool. I always appreciate appreciation!

But it was what she said next that caught my attention. She said that when she goes shopping at the mall, she does whatever she can to avoid eye contact with the sales clerks who approach her asking if they can help. She just wants to get in, make her purchase and get out, and doesn't need the help of some commissioned salesperson trying to sell her something.

How many of you can relate? I can, for sure.

But…what if…instead of avoiding eye contact and communication in these situations, you changed your paradigm and thought of this clerk as a potential client or referral source? Whether she is or is not isn't the point, and we'll get to that shortly. But how would your behavior toward her change if you thought she might create a $10,000 paycheck for you someday? Or how about this—what if you found out she was getting married next month and was going to sell her condo and buy a new home with her new husband, who also had a house to sell?

How would your attitude toward her change?

Guess what? That scenario is entirely possible. Every time you leave the house and encounter other human beings, every single one of them might have a real estate need or know someone who does. Your biggest deal ever. Or, for that matter, your smallest deal ever, which could lead you to your biggest deal ever!

Sure, the majority of people who cross your path on a daily basis have absolutely no use for you as a real estate agent today, tomorrow or next week, whether you're pleasant to them or not. But the problem is, you have no idea which ones do… and which ones don't. And the more pleasant you are to more people, the more likely you are to encounter someone who has a use for you as a real estate agent, right?

"Some salespeople have been taught what is called the "three-foot rule," which says that everyone who comes within three feet is fair game to pitch to about your product.

But what if this person doesn't want to hear about your product? Doesn't she have a choice?

Your first priority in any encounter should be to add value to the other person's life, that is, to enrich or enhance their life in some way. Or at the very least, not to subtract value, which means not to irritate them, suck energy from them, intimidate them, bully them, pressure them or manipulate them.

Great salespeople live by the same code as the physician's oath. First, do no harm.

Part of maturity in sales is coming to grips with the realization that not everyone is a prospective customer, no matter how close to you they may be in feet or in common interests. Great salespeople turn the three-foot rule on its head by making it about the other person. The Go-Giver salesperson's three-foot rule goes something like this:

Anyone within three feet is worth getting to know better."

So, what do I mean by "Pleasant"? Well, Being Pleasant can be as simple as making eye contact and smiling. You can step it up a notch by saying good morning or complimenting their leather jacket. You can take it up another notch by looking for opportunities to open doors for other people, or hold the elevator. You can stop to pet a dog and tell the owner how cute he is (the dog, not the owner!).

What I don't mean by Being Pleasant is going way out of your way to do things for other people. Not that this isn't a fantastic prospecting strategy, but it's not what we're talking about here. When I tell you to Be Pleasant to ten people a day, I'm just telling you to go out in the world without that protective shield around you because you realize that every single person you encounter could be a source of business for you.

Which of course, leads to a few questions, maybe even a few objections.

Are you wondering where to find these ten people?

Are you wondering what to say to these ten people?

Are you wondering how to get contact information for these ten people?

Are you wondering how to tell these ten people you sell real estate without annoying them?

Okay, First, Where Do You Find Ten People a Day to Be Pleasant to?

Well, assuming you leave the house (although you can technically Be Pleasant to people over the phone, too), it's likely you're going places where there are people who will come within three feet of you.

For example, when you're checking out at the grocery store, there are at least four people within three feet of you—the guy behind you, the lady ahead of you, the checkout clerk and the bagger. Maybe the manager wanders by. There you have five people to Be Pleasant to, right there.

If you go to the bank, consider going inside instead of driving-thru—you'll find another three or four or five people there to Be Pleasant to. If you hang out at a coffee shop, don't hide in the back with a book in front of your face; position yourself in the middle of things.

Second, What Do You Say to These Ten People You're Being Pleasant to?

Well, actually, you don't have to make conversation with the ten people, aside from basic pleasantries. I'm certainly not advising you to assault everyone who comes within three feet of you with an elevator speech, or even to comment on their attire. No, the concept is really simple—just Be Pleasant.

Third, How Do You Get Contact Information
for the Ten People?

You won't. The vast majority of the people you're Pleasant to, you'll never see again. You won't be adding them to your SOI database, asking them to lunch or sending them a calendar in December.

But here's the thing. If you're Pleasant to ten people a day, chances are that every few days you'll Be Pleasant to the "right" person and you'll start up a conversation that could lead to a friendship or at least, an acquaintanceship.

Do the math on that and you'll see that by the end of the year, you've Been Pleasant to over 3,000 people and if only one out of ten of them becomes a friend or acquaintance, that's over 300 people you've added to your SOI. Even if your ratio is one of 20 or one of 30, that's some pretty serious SOI-building. *Which doesn't factor in all the people those new friends know and might introduce you to someday.*

But back to the question—how to get contact information from people you meet—you'll do it only if it's appropriate. And it's only appropriate if there's a mutual rapport and both parties seem interested in continuing the relationship. Do not go out in the world Being Pleasant with the goal of gathering names and numbers. You'll sabotage yourself.

Last, How Do You Tell These Ten People You Sell Real Estate?

Again, you probably won't. Don't make it your goal; if you get to the point with someone that you're talking at the level of "So, what do you do?" then you'll tell them. But don't lead with it and don't insist on fitting it into the conversation if it's not appropriate.

So, Jennifer, tell me again why I'm Being Pleasant to Ten People a Day?

Well, in order to increase the number of human beings on the planet who know you, like you, and know that you sell real estate, you need to meet people. And meeting people is not nearly as difficult and complicated as we like to make it. You don't have to join clubs or volunteer at the homeless shelter or join a networking group or do anything you don't want to do, just to "meet people."

People to meet are all around you. And if you're Pleasant to more of them, you'll meet more of them.

The Karma of Being Pleasant

So, how does this Being Pleasant sound so far? Pretty good? It gets better! We haven't yet talked about the general good karma and reciprocal Pleasantness that will result from all your Pleasantness. Imagine if you have ten positive encounters every day with other human beings as opposed to neutral or even negative ones—what do you reckon that might do for your mood? And have you ever noticed that when you're in a good mood, good things seem to find you? That you seem to find more and more things to be in a good mood about?

"But, Jennifer, I AM pleasant to everyone I meet and I don't remember ever getting business from it!"

Well, that may very well be. But before we accept this statement at face value, let's…not.

First, very few people think they're UNpleasant to the people they encounter in their day-to-day wanderings. Hopefully they're right—that they don't intentionally put a damper on the moods of the other human beings who cross their paths. Sure, we all have our bad days and we certainly run into people out there in the world who deserve our being UNpleasant to them, but in general, I believe that most of us intend to make the world a brighter place when we're out in it.

But do we? Ask any grocery store check-out clerk how many customers look her in the eye when she greets them. How many smile and return the greeting sincerely. And don't forget the story that began this chapter—my reader who purposely avoids eye contact and extraneous conversation when shopping at the mall (and many of us admitted doing the same thing). I don't know about you, but when I'm at Walmart, I avert my gaze when I meet someone in the shampoo aisle and pretend I'm completely unaware of their presence.

Next time you're out in public, be it at Walmart, Sam's Club, Home Depot or the Piggly-Wiggly, pay close attention to how you interact with the other people you find there. Do you make eye contact and smile? Do you acknowledge their existence at all? Do you do anything that might make them feel just a teeny bit special, or just a little bit happier than they were before they encountered you?

Note...

Of course, nothing in this advice includes leering, flirting, stalking or otherwise making other people uncomfortable with your attention, or putting yourself in any danger. I'll trust your good judgment and common sense not to overdo your Being Pleasant to the point where your victim calls security, or you feel you're sending the wrong message.

Are you wondering how Being Pleasant will get you business?

Well, it might not, directly. You probably won't venture out into the world Being Pleasant and come home with a signed listing agreement or a hot new buyer. On the other hand, you might. But remember, the goal isn't to go out there finding prospects and clients; it's to expand your sphere of influence by getting to know more people...and you never know who among your new friends will lead you to your next $10,000 paycheck. Read on.

INTERLUDE: IS IT MERCENARY TO "USE" YOUR SPHERE OF INFLUENCE FOR BUSINESS?

I often toss around the phrase "You never know who might lead you to your next $10,000 paycheck." What I mean is that in our business, we get big paychecks when we perform. And since most people you're going to meet either own or know someone who owns or wants to own real property, most people you're going to meet can potentially be or introduce you to your next client.

I've always been pretty transparent as to my "mercenariness" about my social life. Before I went into real estate, I didn't have a lot of friends. Didn't bother me at all; I've never been all that socially inclined and am usually happy to stay home at night and watch Survivor. But when I hung my shiny new real estate license on the wall of my new office, and was made aware that I was going to have to drum up business for myself, it suddenly occurred to me that having more friends might help me do that.

And I was right. As soon as I had a "reason" to have a social life, I went out and got myself one. And in the process, discovered the joys of having friends, of having plans, of having people in my life who care about me, and I about them.

But yes, there was also joy in having those friends hire me and refer business to me.

I'd like to say that my conversion from functional hermit to social butterfly as a result of my real estate career has stuck with me, even now that I'm no longer selling real estate. But it hasn't. Now that my livelihood is based more on the hours I spend at my keyboard than on the hours I spend with friends, that's what I do. Spend hours on my keyboard, that is, instead of being out in the world with my antenna up hoping to make new friends. As I write this, I've lived in Florida 18 months and can count on my fingers and toes how many people I know here.

But I digress.

Back to the original question: IS it mercenary to intentionally expand your social network so that you can make more money?

Sure it is. But so what? Assuming you're selling real estate in hopes of making money, you have to go get yourself some buyers and sellers. And "use" them to make money from. Whether your clients come from traditional prospecting methods like cold-calling, door-knocking, open-housing or mass-mailing, or from throwing a party, going to lunch or Being Pleasant to people, your prospecting efforts are done with the intention of getting business from those efforts.

But here's the kicker.

If you follow the principles of **Selling** with Soul, you're providing more in value to your clients than they are providing to you in paychecks. You are a fantastic real estate agent and you are horrified by the thought that anyone you know would hire or refer anyone but you. Not because you need that paycheck or your feelings might be hurt, but because you're the best real estate agent you know. And you'd hate to see anyone you know hire or refer someone who won't do as wonderful a job as you will. That's just not right!

Further, if you're following the principles of **Prospecting** with Soul, your promotional efforts with the people you know won't annoy, irritate or bother them a bit. Whatever you do to remind your sphere of influence that you exist will be of value and interest to them, not all about you. It's a win/win.

Hey, you gotta get business from someone, so in that regard, you're "using" everyone who hires you to be their real estate agent. But if you feel in your heart and soul that you're the best thing that could ever happen to your clients, you'll have no qualms about it!

"Exposure plus 95 cents might buy you a decent cup of coffee. The key is to 'position' yourself in your market as the expert, the resource, the only person your prospect would ever even THINK of doing business with, or referring to others."
—Bob Burg

CHAPTER SIX

Attracting Business by Mastering Your Market

YOU may be wondering why I'm including a chapter about becoming a master of your market in a book specifically called *PROSPECT with Soul*. After all, sure, knowing your market is a dandy thing for a real estate agent, but what does it have to do with prospecting?

Ahhhhh…that's what we're going to talk about here. How and why being a market master helps you prospect. And how to become one of those—a market master, that is.

Before I continue, I hope you're not asking yourself why it's important to know your market. Even if I'm completely, utterly full of it that knowing your market can be a great prospecting strategy, there's really no debate that as real estate agents, our primary product is property knowledge and it's important that we thoroughly understand our product.

Those who have been selling real estate a while may take the importance of knowing their market for granted, but as someone who has relocated from one market to another—the first market being one I knew everything about and the second being one I knew nothing about—I can tell you that knowing your market compared to not knowing your market is far more comfortable. It's crazy-UNcomfortable to try to sound as if you know what you're doing as a real estate agent if you don't know much about the real estate market. Once you've experienced the pleasure of being a master of your market, you can't imagine doing this business without that knowledge.

But, also…it's a really, really good prospecting strategy to have that knowledge.

What Does It Mean to Be a Master of Your Market?

When I refer to being a Master of Your Market, what do I mean by that?

Well, for me, knowing my market means several things. First, that I am able to be casually conversational about it. If the opportunity arises to talk about real estate, say, at an open house or on floor time or with a sign caller or even at a party, I sound as if I know what I'm talking about, without having to look at MLS print-outs or market reports. And I sound as if I know what I'm talking about because I do know what I'm talking about. Not just facts and figures and statistics; I have a true understanding of what's happening in my market.

It also means that if someone tells me where they live, I get a mental image of their neighborhood or subdivision or condo building. I don't necessarily know exactly what year their house was built, although I might be able to guess fairly accurately, but I have a general sense of the overall ambience of the area, what amenities are nearby, and I probably have a personal anecdote or two about the area I can toss out.

Conversely, "not knowing a market" means that if someone tells me where they live and it's outside of my area of expertise, I probably can't come up with much that's intelligent to say beyond—"*Oh, yeah…um…my friend Patty lives over there.*" Or, "*How nice, I've heard it's beautiful there.*" Basic small-talk, really.

There's nothing wrong with not "knowing a market" because you can't be an expert everywhere—that sort of negates the concept of being an expert, but obviously, the more familiar you are with more areas and property types in your market, the more often you'll be able to build rapport with potential clients.

So, that's what I mean by being a master of your market. Not that you have a whole bunch of statistics and data and facts and figures memorized, but that you can speak intelligently, confidently and knowledgeably about the local real estate market or, depending on the size of your market, segments of it.

How Can Being a Master of Your Market Get You Business?

But back to the main point of this chapter. How can being a master of your market help you, to put it bluntly, get more business?

Well, remember, real estate business comes from people. Real live human beings. Whether these real live human beings are already friends or acquaintances of yours, or if they're total strangers to you, it doesn't matter, they are people.

My, Jennifer, you have such a profound grasp of the obvious…

Thank you ☺

These people have the potential to hire you or refer you to others and they have to make a decision about whether or not they're going to do that. And that decision will likely be based on some sort of conversation between the two of you. And in that conversation, somehow you have to inspire them to think of you as a real estate agent worth hiring or referring to. Or, at the very least, inspire them to take an interest in you and your real estate career so you'll have the opportunity to show them how wonderful you are when the time is right.

Do you see where I'm going with this?

As a real estate agent, what do you have to offer the world's people—those individual human beings you'll be having conversations with—that might inspire them to take an interest in you as a real estate agent?

Do these people-in-the-world care about your gorgeous home brochures? Do they really want to hear about your 32-step marketing plan? Do they want to hear about your agent of the month award? Do they want to be added to your newsletter mailing list?

Honestly? Probably not, at least not right off the bat. But I'll bet you a lot of them would be interested in how houses are selling in their neck of the woods or about that underpriced duplex you previewed that morning or which neighborhoods are recovering faster than others and why. If a person, friend or stranger has any interest at all in the current real estate market and you can confidently make intelligent conversation about it, you'll get him, if he's gettable.

Compare that to the response of *"Well, I'm not sure about that, but I'd be happy to find out for you"* when the topic of real estate comes up. Just doesn't have quite the same ring, does it?

This applies regardless of where you meet these people you're having conversations with. For example, let's say you meet someone at an open house. If the best you can do is hand a visitor a list of other homes in the neighborhood, but can't really make conversation about the houses on the list, the possibility of watching that stranger walk back out your door just went way up. But if you can easily chatter about nearby listings or comparable neighborhoods, you just dramatically increased the chances that your visitor will ask for your business card. (See Chapter Eight about Open Houses.)

When you're on floor time or take a sign call, again, if you can speak intelligently about the market either surrounding your listing or that your office specializes in, you'll easily capture those leads. (See Chapter Seven – Floor Time, Sign Calls and Internet Inquiries.)

If you read *Sell with Soul*, you might remember my story of shopping for my own piece of real estate in South Florida. The short version is that I wandered into a real estate office in Ft. Lauderdale and was given to Judy, the agent on floor duty. To put it bluntly, Judy knew nothing about her market and wasted two hours of my time (and energy) trying to look up properties for me on the MLS. She couldn't answer my basic question of, given my price range, could I afford to live on or near the beach?

The next day, I visited a RE/MAX office in Naples and spoke with Jim who knew everything about his local market. In 15 minutes, he was able to tell me what was available on or near the beach and, sadly, to gently break the news to me that the beach was way out of my price range.

So, imagine Judy, the first agent, at a party, and the subject of real estate comes up. Because Judy's office is near the beach, maybe someone asks her about the vacation condo market, I dunno, maybe they ask if "vacation condos cash-flow and about how much do they cost?" Do you think Judy would have been able to draw that person in and inspire them to trust her with their business or referrals? Probably not. Conversely, what if Jim was at a party in Naples and someone asked him the same question? He's got 'em.

Mastering Your Market by Memorizing the MLS?

Don't try to master a market by studying the MLS. No amount of research sitting behind your desk comes close to the knowledge you'll gain by actually looking at property and neighborhoods. If you make physically previewing properties a priority in your business life, you can learn a market, or at least segments of it, pretty quickly. Remember earlier I said that my definition of being a market expert is the ability to visualize a neighborhood when someone gives me an address? Well, there's no way you can develop that level of familiarity from just researching the MLS.

Some real estate trainers encourage agents to study and even memorize what they call "relevant statistics," like Days on Market and Price per Square Foot and Average List-to-Sold ratios and absorption rates and such.

I disagree. While such statistics might be of interest to you, it's not likely they'll be all that interesting to those people you're out there hopefully having conversations with. And without a conversational familiarity with the actual neighborhoods and homes and local amenities, this data is going to be even more uninteresting to the average Joe if you try to have a conversation with Joe about it.

And besides, cold hard numbers are meaningless indicators of the real estate market if the person spouting the numbers can't relate those numbers to what's really happening.

For example, if the average Days on Market (DOM) in a neighborhood is 102 days, what does that really mean?

Well, it could mean two different things, right?

It might mean that some houses sell in 2 days and some in 200 days, for an average DOM of 102. In fact, there may not be one house in the last six months that sold in exactly 102 days. It's entirely possible; in fact, that half the houses sold in the first 30 days and the other half took six months, which would result in a DOM somewhere in the middle.

But it's also possible that the DOM statistic of 102 days actually means that most houses in that area typically take three to four months to sell. So, part of knowing your market is knowing whether or not the average DOM is relevant or not.

The same with list-to-sold price. You'll probably see a range of list-to-sold percentages from 0% to 30% off the list price. If that's the case, it's misleading to average those percentages and say that "houses are selling at 92% of asking."

The problem is, the general public thinks that these statistics are relevant and if you can't spit out something satisfying to this belief, your audience will think you don't know your stuff. And the time usually isn't right to give a little lesson on the differences between average and median and mean prices or marketing days. So what do you do if someone asks you for statistics?

"So, Jennifer, what's the average days on market these days?"

This is where understanding your market is far more important than memorizing it. You can politely evade the question and draw the person in if you paint a picture of the market instead. For example, I'd probably say something like, *"Oh, gosh, it depends on the day and price range and the style of home, but overall, great houses that are priced right sell quickly—under a week sometimes even. But there is a lot of inventory and if a house isn't one of the best available, it may sit for months and months and may not even sell at all."*

How Do You Become a Market Master?

Oh, my, let us count the ways!

First, if it's customary to preview in your market, do that. A lot. If you're not familiar with "previewing," it simply means to go look at listed houses by yourself or with another agent, not with a buyer. Some markets frown on previewing and if that's the case in yours, you might want to move. Just kidding, sort of. I advise all new agents to spend some serious quality time previewing in their first few months on the job. Like every other day if they can.

In order to be an effective previewer, you need to practice what I call "Opinionated Previewing" or "Previewing with a Purpose." When you go out to look at houses with the goal of learning your market, you should look at homes that you can compare to each other. A great example of opinionated previewing is when you preview in preparation for an open house. You're looking for other somewhat similar homes to the home you're holding open so that you can speak intelligently to visitors about the competition for this home. Or, of course, if you're previewing for a new buyer, you'll be looking for the best homes to show him in a price range. Or, heck, maybe you just want to get a feel for what your own house is worth, so you go out and look at homes like yours. Whatever your excuse, being able to compare homes to each other helps you internalize the data you're gathering.

Another way to learn more about your market is to always have your antenna up for opportunities to show properties to buyers. Even buyers who probably won't ever lead you to a paycheck. While I won't talk here about what a great prospecting strategy it can be to be willing to Waste Your Time with low-priority prospects, I will say that it's a fantastic way to build your market expertise. It's one thing for you to go out alone and preview, but quite another to have someone else with you to provide feedback on what you're seeing. And if you make conversation with this person, you'll get to hear their impressions of neighborhoods and styles and features, which will help you better understand what's important to the consumer.

So, go ahead and drive across town for a sign call. Do a market analysis for a friend who is just looking for help protesting his tax assessment. Go on listing appointments even if you're pretty sure the seller is just "using" you for information. Take a buyer out to look at properties even if she says she won't buy till next spring.

If you live in or near a resort area, make sure you can speak intelligently about the highly desirable properties—for example, how much does a beachfront home or condo cost, or how much will a buyer have to pay to be on the slopes or on the lake? Even if that's not really your niche, I'm sure you'd be happy to sell a beachfront home or ski-in/ski-out condo, right?

Choosing a Market to Master

How do you pick the area or areas you want to become an expert in? Well, of course, that's your choice! You might deliberately choose to work a certain market or property type, or you may find yourself with an expertise you didn't plan on. It will probably be a combination of both. Your own neighborhood is a great place to start, or the neighborhood your office specializes in. My specialty had always been the historic neighborhoods of Central Denver as well as the close-in alternatives to these neighborhoods for buyers who wanted Charming Old Denver but couldn't afford it.

Don't try to specialize in an area or property type that you don't like. For example, in my second year I worked in a suburban office and tried to get into the inventory but just couldn't. I didn't understand the buyer or the seller, and frankly, I really didn't care to. I also tried to work in the foothills outside of Denver and it wasn't a good fit for me either. I'd look at houses priced at $500,000 and ones priced at $1.5M and couldn't tell the difference.

The job of "becoming" a market master is never really done. Markets change (duh) and in order to truly be a master, you have to keep up with the changes. Don't go overboard—you do have other things to do besides preview (I hope!), but try to keep Market Mastery on your to-do list. You'll feel awfully smart the next time you capture a great new client at a party because you knew how much that Victorian down the street sold for!

"In about the same degree that you are helpful, you will be happy."
—Karl Reiland

CHAPTER SEVEN

Floor Time, Sign Calls & Internet Inquiries

I'M grouping these three distinct categories of prospecting strategies into one chapter because, as different as they may appear on the surface, they're all best approached with the same attitude!

To briefly define each…"Floor Time" (also called "floor duty," "desk duty," "opportunity time," or "up-time") is when you make yourself available at your office (or in virtual offices, accessible by phone) to talk with people who either stop by the office or call in asking for a real estate agent. If you're "on floor," you'll get the lead to do with what you will—hopefully turn him into a prospect and eventually a client. In many offices, floor time is voluntary, that is, you aren't required to do it; busy agents with established sources of business rarely take floor while newer agents often do (and should).

"Sign Calls" are phone calls you receive because your For Sale sign is in someone's yard, that is, someone sees your sign on one of your listings and calls you for more information or to schedule a time to look at it.

"Internet Inquiries" (not to be confused with Internet leads, see Chapter Fourteen – From Online Lead to Real World Client) are emails you receive from people who saw your listing online at websites like REALTOR.com, or on your own website or blog.

Floor Time

If you need business, there's no downside to volunteering for floor time, and plenty of upside. First, your broker will see that you're working, and may be more willing to toss you a lead from time to time if he feels you're committed to your success. You'll be more likely to get to know other agents in the office who, while not technically among your SOI, can, like your broker, be a decent source of leads if they ever find themselves a little overwhelmed. Likewise, the receptionist will get to know you better and may consider you to be her go-to guy or gal when leads come in during times when there isn't anyone scheduled for floor duty.

Of course, the real reason to "do" floor is to gather leads. Whether or not floor time is productive for you will depend on many factors, not the least of which is the quantity of call-ins and walk-ins your office enjoys. If your office is in a busy shopping district, your floor time may be tremendous; if it's in a high-rise building, perhaps not so much.

But your attitude toward call-ins and walk-ins and your behavior toward them can make a world of difference in how many you convert to prospects and clients.

Before I get into a discussion of your attitude and behavior ☺, let me talk for a moment about, ho hum, market knowledge.

I know I beat on this drum incessantly, but that's 'cause it's a really important drum! In order to be effective on floor duty, you must be able to speak intelligently about your market. Specifically about the market your office focuses on since that'll be what callers and visitors will most likely be interested in. If your office is near the ski resort, you need to be conversant about properties on and near the slopes. If your office is in your downtown financial district, you need to know about downtown lofts, condos and apartments. If it's in a fancy-schmantzy shopping district, you'll need to be familiar with properties within walking distance to the shops and restaurants.

We just talked about this in the last chapter, so I won't repeat myself here, but I couldn't let an opportunity slip by to encourage you to Master Your Market.

Be Helpful!

I'll assume you already have a conversational familiarity with the market your office advertises to; let's get back to your attitude and behavior toward people who call or come in the office during your floor shift.

Approach your visitor with an attitude of helpfulness. Don't even think about withholding information because they haven't yet committed to you; freely give, give, give whatever you can. Many agents believe that if they give away too much information, their target will take that information and run with it, because they no longer "need" them.

But in most cases, that's simply not true. Raw information is no longer difficult to find—anyone can go online and get information on just about anything—but knowing exactly what to do with the information is a whole 'nother thing. In the vast majority of circumstances, your cheerfully providing good information will only serve to demonstrate your expertise and enhance your credibility with the potential client rather than send him on his way now that he's picked your brain and doesn't need you anymore.

If you truly know your stuff and you know that you know your stuff, that knowledge is magnetic to the person you're sharing it with. And the best way to demonstrate that you do know your stuff is to freely share your knowledge with others. Just telling someone that you're an expert isn't nearly as convincing!

What Is the Buyer Looking for?

Okay, so a potential buyer walks in the door and ends up sitting across the conference room table from you. What's next?

Well, some trainers would have you whipping out your Buyer Questionnaire and ~~interrogating~~ interviewing your ~~victim~~ buyer prospect as to exactly what he's looking for in what timeframe at what price range and oh, yeah, if he's approved for a loan and oh, yeah some more, here's an exclusive buyer agency agreement that requires your signature.

No, no, no. That's just wrong. All of it.

Calm down. Breathe. This person is a guest in your office, so be polite and make him feel welcome. Warmly introduce yourself. Offer some coffee or water. Once you're comfortably settled in, just make conversation with him as you would with anyone you were having a conversation with!

Calmly ask him what sort of home he's looking for. Take notes if you like, but it's not necessary at this point. Let him talk. Ask questions from time to time, but no interrogation or formal questionnaire, please. There's plenty of time (or not) for that later. Right now your goal is to build rapport and trust, and, soon, to demonstrate your expertise. Rapport and trust are best built through listening, not talking!

Here's all you really need to know during this first conversation:

1. What sort of property he's looking for
2. What type of neighborhood he's interested in
3. If he has a price range in mind
4. What his general timeframe is
5. If there is any very specific must-have on his list (e.g., school district, RV parking, non-restrictive zoning)

You don't need to ask exactly how many bedrooms and bathrooms he wants. Whether or not he needs a garage. What his minimum square footage requirements are. Not even whether or not he's spoken to a lender.

Again, there's plenty of time for that. Don't chase him off at this early stage before he's grown to like and trust you.

You Don't Need a Questionnaire

So you've built a little rapport and the buyer seems to want to move forward. **Is now** the time to whip out the Buyer Questionnaire?

No. Frankly, I'm not a fan of buyer questionnaires at all. I believe you can discover everything you need to know about a buyer from having a regular conversation with him. And if you can't remember the things you need to know from a buyer without your Questionnaire, well, um…that's scary.

Jennifer's $0.02

Many agents have been "burned" by buyer prospects who took an hour of their time and then vanished. The solution these agents come up with to avoid this happening in the future is to enforce sterner "rules" on any prospect who stumbles in the door to "ensure" the agent's time isn't wasted again. I believe, in the vast majority of these cases, the agent already came on too strong and scared the buyer off. Relationships, even business relationships, take time. Yes, your time is valuable, but spending MORE time with a potential $10,000 paycheck instead of less time is probably an excellent use of your time.

The problem with questionnaires aside from the fact that you don't need them is that they're way too comprehensive.

Huh? What do you mean, "too" comprehensive?

Most people don't buy houses very often, so they don't really know what they want aside from a very few Must-Have criteria (and even those are subject to change). Believe it or not, it can be counterproductive to attempt to nail down exactly what a buyer is looking for because he doesn't know! But if you force him to answer your questions, he might make up answers just to please you.

Why is that a problem? Well, you might end up ruling out homes that the buyer would have liked but that didn't quite fit what he said he wanted during your interview. Another possibility is that you create expectations in your buyer's mind that you can't possibly fulfill given his price range or location preferences.

Anyway, back to your **conversation** (not interrogation). Depending on the buyer's schedule, a good next step might be to open up your laptop, log into your MLS and do a preliminary search for your buyer while he's sitting right there. As you're inputting his parameters, you can ask for his minimum number of bedrooms and baths, if having a garage is a necessity and a handful of other common filters. Use the price range he gives you without question and, together, review the listings that come up.

If you're familiar enough with your market, you might be able to comment on some of the homes, either because you've been inside them or you are familiar with their location. For example, you might be able to say, "*Ooooh, that's a nice one. The bedrooms are a little small, but the kitchen is fabulous.*" Or "*That one's on a really busy street—would that be a problem for you?*"

These little comments will do wonders to demonstrate your expertise and knowledge of the market. You don't have to know every listing in town, of course, but it will sound as if you do!

At this point, you should have built enough of a relationship with the buyer prospect to push for the next step.

Which is…buyer agency, right?

Buyer Agency?

Nope. Not on my watch, anyway. Yes, the buyer might think you're a decent guy or gal at this point, but that's about it. You haven't yet earned the right of asking the buyer for the honor of his commitment to you; you're just scratching the surface of establishing trust.

No, the next step in my book (*which this happens to be*) is to schedule a time to go look at houses together. I'll let you take it from here. For more advice on working with buyers, read Chapter Eight in *Sell with Soul* and/or Chapter Six in FUN.

Voices from the Real World of Real Estate

Contributed by Susan Haughton (www.susanmovesyou.com)

A couple of years ago, I met with a couple who had been referred to me by a previous client. When they walked into the office, he was carrying a notebook and several books, one of which was "Real Estate for Dummies." Oh, boy.

The first words out of the husband's mouth were, "I'm not signing any kind of agreement or contract to work with you."

I just chuckled and said, "Oh, don't worry. I haven't decided if I want to work with you, either."

His wife burst out laughing (whew!).

I continued, "We need to see if it's a good fit; I want you to have confidence in me because of my abilities and because I am going to do a great job for you. Right now, you have no clue about that, do you?"

"Well," he hesitated, "Jonathan did tell me what a good job you did for him."

"Yeah, there's that. But this is about you and what makes you comfortable. So, let's talk about you guys."

I have a love/hate relationship with the exclusive buyer agency agreement...I don't love it, I don't hate it and, to be honest, I have only used it when a client requested it.

Yes, that's right, I have had clients request it because they read about it somewhere and thought they needed it. It's okay, I'm happy to give you one, as long as it has an expiration date that doesn't string us both out too terribly long.

Ah, why the attitude, you may ask.

Simple.

I don't want to be contractually obligated to someone who is prone to cheat on me. That's akin to marrying the guy who is texting your best friend behind your back... seriously, he's already showing signs of bad faith, so why would you want to force him into a monogamous relationship for which he is clearly not ready?

There are plenty of good guys out there, so why on earth would I want to be tied up with one that isn't right for me?

And isn't that what we're really talking about here? Trying to lock in a client's loyalty with a piece of paper?

I look for clients with whom I have great rapport, clients who respect my knowledge, experience and work ethic. I look for motivated clients who take the process seriously and who are committed to the home buying or selling process. Clients who trust me to do a good job for them.

If I don't sense it is going to be a good fit and the relationship is not going to be a mutually satisfying one, then I'm the first to say it's time for a change.

Floor <u>Calls</u> (versus floor walk-ins)

What if your floor duty lead "comes in" on the phone? That is, he or she calls the office with a question about one of the office listings, or about real estate in general?

Similar "rules" apply. Be helpful. Very helpful. Be pleasant. Very pleasant. No pressure. No sales pitch. No nosy questions about loan approval or credit-worthiness. Behave as if the person on the other end of the phone line might be, or lead you to, your biggest client ever. Don't push for an appointment, but you might try saying something like *"Well, if you haven't found a great real estate agent to help you yet, I'd be happy to meet with you and see if I might fit the bill!"*

A little reverse psychology can work wonders here, too. If it seems appropriate, you can use the *"of course you'll want to shop around"* strategy described earlier. "Assume" the buyer already has a real estate agent by saying something like, *"Have you seen many houses yet with your agent?"* If he has an agent, he'll answer honestly. If he doesn't, he'll probably also answer honestly, and you can take it from there.

Jennifer's $0.02

Should you drop everything for a walk-in or call-in buyer who wants to see houses Right Now? Probably not. Too much risk, both personally and professionally. While it's highly unlikely a serial killer is going to stumble into your real estate office, there's no good (enough) reason to take that chance. And professionally, while being enthusiastic and flexible are good things, appearing desperate for business is not. Besides, unless you are extremely familiar with the inventory, you take the chance of looking inexperienced or incompetent if you don't have time to prepare for your showings.

Seller Floor Leads

Before we leave the topic of Floor Time, let's talk a minute or two about seller walk-ins and call-ins.

If someone calls or drops by the office interested in talking to an agent about listing their home, the process is a bit different. Yes, you still want to build rapport, but it's okay to use more of a questionnaire approach. Not literally—you don't have to have a questionnaire in hand—but it's fine to ask a series of questions without the risk of coming on too strong.

Here's how I might proceed with a seller walk-in/call-in.

"Okay, let's talk about your house. What's the address?"

<seller responds. If you can look up the address in your MLS or tax records, do this as you're talking>

"Okay, tell me about the house."

<the seller will tell you the basics: bedrooms, baths, approximate square footage. Feel free to let him talk as long as he wants. If he leaves anything out, such as the existence or size of the garage, give him a nudge, but otherwise, just listen and take notes>

"What's your timeframe, do you think?"

<seller responds>

"Okay, I think I have a good picture of the situation to get started—can I come see the house later today?"

<seller responds>

It could go anywhere from here. The seller may want to talk about your commission or your marketing plan or he may simply invite you over. I'll refer you to Chapters Seven, Eight and Ten in FUN for further discussion on effective listing presentations, including a full discussion of commission negotiation.

All this said, don't get too wrapped up in following any particular script or dialogue or process. These are people. Just talk to them. You'll hit it off better with some than others and that's okay. You won't win 'em all and that's also okay. Some days you'll be in the zone and some days you won't. And that's okay.

Every time you meet with a buyer or seller prospect, you'll learn something to take to your next meeting with a buyer or seller prospect. And trust me—the learning process never ends, even if you sell real estate for the next 50 years. At least, I hope it doesn't!

Sign Calls

Much of what you just read applies, in pieces and parts, to soulfully handling "sign calls."

When someone calls from a For Sale sign, they're usually interested in the house it's sitting in front of. So, cheerfully answer any questions the caller has about the house and if she seems interested, offer to show it to her. At no time should you make any sort of overture as to whether or not she's in the market for a real estate agent. Just be awfully darn helpful and nice. If she wants to see the house, schedule a time to meet her there and show it. No sales pitch whatsoever from you. Don't make her come to your office first. This will differentiate you from the other agents she's calling from signs, all of whom are either rudely brushing her off or prematurely pressuring her for an exclusive agreement.

When you meet face to face at the house, if the two of you are hitting it off, casually start talking about the real estate market in general, and the neighborhood you're in specifically. Demonstrate your market knowledge by mentioning other recent sales or active listings. Ask if she's seen a lot of homes or if she's just starting the search. If she tells you she's seen quite a few, ask *"Oh, who's your real estate agent?"* as if you're sure she already has one and have no designs on sales-pitching her at all. It's often at this point she'll open up and tell you how unhappy she is with her current agent, or how frustrated she's been trying to find the right agent for her. Just smile sympathetically and BAM! She's yours. Okay, well, not every time, but often enough!

Internet Inquiries

When you get Internet inquiries, respond promptly and answer the person's questions cheerfully and thoroughly. Don't try to coerce them into an appointment until they broach the subject themselves or seem open to your doing it. Be overly generous with your advice—I can't tell you how much good will this will generate with your audience. And I can see why—I myself have contacted gurus hoping to pick their brains on some matter or other and have been brusquely referred to their "purchase-my-time" page, or quickly informed of their hourly consulting rate. BEFORE I was convinced I even wanted or needed their advice! Maybe these guys know something I don't about time management, but personally I'd rather spend a little time helping someone realize how wonderful I am than shoo them away if they haven't opened their checkbook in the first five minutes.

As with sign calls, people who email you about a listing are also emailing agents all over town. If you don't pressure them or otherwise make them uncomfortable (or, worse, ignore them!), you'll stand out from the crowd.

The punch line here is that whenever you answer the phone, open your email or meet with an office drop-in and find yourself chatting with a potential customer, strive to be helpful and pleasant instead of striving to qualify. If someone walks into your office and wants help, be helpful. Restrain yourself from any sales-pitching or agreement-signing.

Approach this person as you would like to be approached if you called-in, walked-in or emailed-in to a real estate office in search of help. It really is that simple!

"Whatever job you take on, make yourself valuable, then indispensable."
—Brian Tracy

Open Houses

THE open house. THE go-to activity for real estate agents in need of some business!

On the off-chance you have no idea what I'm talking about, in most markets, real estate agents consider open houses to be primarily a prospecting activity, not a home-selling activity. I have some issues with this philosophy, but I've yammered on enough about them on other platforms, and this really isn't the appropriate one.

Anyway, real estate agents, especially newer ones, will "do" an open house on a Saturday or Sunday afternoon, hoping to snag some buyers, maybe even a seller or two. They assume, reasonably so, that a visitor who shows up at the open house does so because he has at least a passing interest in real estate and maybe, just maybe, doesn't yet have a real estate agent to help him.

There are all sorts of strategies to capture these buyers and sellers—from requiring sign-in when they walk in the door to offering helpful doo-dads to providing free market information to offering to show them other available listings in the event "this one doesn't quite work."

The goal of these strategies is to get the potential buyer's or seller's contact information so the agent can track them down and give 'em her best sales pitch. The

Chapter Eight: **Open Houses**   101

eventual goal being, of course, to seduce them into hiring her to be their buyer (or seller) agent.

All good stuff! After all, the premise that someone visiting an open house is more likely to be in need or want of real estate assistance than some random someone off the street is perfectly valid. And if that someone needs a real estate agent, it might as well be you, right?

Right!

But many agents shy away from pushing themselves on open house visitors because they realize (also correctly) that these poor visitors are already being pushed upon by the agents holding open the other houses they've visited! And, being the soulful sorts they are, are hesitant to do something unto another that would annoy them if done unto them.

And God Bless 'em for that.

So, what's a soulful agent to do?

Before I answer that burning question, let me tell you a story.

A few months ago, I had a conversation with a newer agent about maximizing the effectiveness of her open houses. By "effectiveness," of course, she meant gathering as many names, numbers and email addresses as she could during her three-hour stint on a Sunday afternoon.

She was frustrated (mostly with herself) at her inability to smoothly gather those names, numbers and email addresses from her visitors. Either her visitors seemed hesitant to provide them OR she just wasn't comfortable asking, and usually came away from her open houses empty-handed.

"Jennifer—do you have any suggestions for me?"

As a matter of fact, I do.

First, let's have a paradigm shift, shall we? Too often, we real estate agents focus on what WE need and want, and hope to persuade our audience to play along. For example, WE want that name, number and email address so WE can send a nice little thank-you-for-visiting note and add a warm body to our mailing list, right?

So we come up with all sorts of sly strategies to get that contact information, such as, *"the seller asks that guests sign in for security purposes"* or, *"if you register, you'll be entered to win a lovely gift basket"* or simply, *"please sign my register so I can show the seller how many visitors we had."*

Nothing really wrong with these approaches except that there's nothing in it for the visitor. At least, nothing worth relinquishing private contact information to a hungry real estate agent, suspecting they'll be hounded after the fact whether they want to be or not.

So, what could you do instead to—**here's the kicker**—INSPIRE the visitor to want you to have his or her contact information? Not what you can do to trick it out of him, but to actually inspire him to want to give it to you?

And no, the answer isn't to bribe him with free reports, contests, drawings or newsletters…

Any ideas?

A Real World Open House Success Story

I think back to the very first open house I ever visited, before I was in possession of my own bright shiny real estate license. One Sunday afternoon, I was driving around a neighborhood in my new home city of Denver, pre-approval in hand for a loan up to $119,000. Oh, it was an exciting time.

I stopped in front of a house with a big OPEN HOUSE sandwich board prominently displayed on the sidewalk. Walked in, was greeted by a friendly real estate agent named Melody. Melody gave me a brochure and invited me to look around. I did. I liked what I saw. I expressed my enthusiasm to Melody, who smiled. She agreed that it was, indeed, a fine house, but unfortunately there were already multiple offers on it; she was just holding it open because she'd advertised the open house in the paper and didn't want to be a no-show.

Well, bummer. I really liked the house.

"Well," said Melody, *"have you seen the one at 3943 Vallejo? It's similar to this one, but has a second bath. There's another nice home in this price range at 4401 Clay and it has a garage! And my office has a new listing coming up this week sometime that has…"*

My eyes lit up. All was not lost? There were other houses as wonderful as this one? And this magical all-knowing creature could help me get one for myself?

Oh, yes, Melody assured me. There were indeed other wonderful houses and she would be absolutely delighted to help me get one for myself.

I excitedly offered my name and phone number to Melody without her even asking for them. I was happy to do so and she, of course, was happy to take them. She said she had to finish up her open house, but would contact me later with more information.

(Keep in mind this was before the era of online MLS listings, so I was truly dependent on Melody for that information. It's different today, obviously, but the philosophy is the same).

I raced home and literally waited by the phone to hear from Melody. And, lo and behold, the phone rang! It was her! As promised!

Melody showed me several houses and I bought one fairly quickly. Over the next two years I bought three more, using Melody as my agent.

So, how did Melody get my precious contact information and, later, my loyal business (before I got my own real estate license, that is)? Did she coerce me into providing it with promises of lovely gift baskets or free market reports? Did she risk offending me with a request to sign in "for security purposes"?

None of the above.

She inspired me to give her my contact information because she had something I truly wanted. Information. Expertise. Access. And we hit it off well enough during our conversation for me to be able to envision myself working with her (that's important and we'll talk about it in a bit).

Today's open house visitor may not be as uninformed and naïve as I was, but that doesn't change the concept. Your goal when prospecting at an open house is not to pry conversation and contact information from an unwilling visitor; it's to (here's that word again) <u>inspire</u> him or her to want to talk with you, both today and in the future.

So, how d'ya do that? How do you inspire a perfect stranger to think of you as someone they'd like to hear from again?

Well, first, I hope it was obvious from the Melody story that, as we discussed earlier, having a conversational familiarity with the immediate neighborhood is huge. Projecting a confident, yet casual air of being a neighborhood expert is probably the best way to turn open house visitors into buyer clients.

It also helps to have a reasonable familiarity with other similar neighborhoods to offer as alternatives to visitors if they find that this particular neighborhood is too expensive for their budget (which is quite common—open house visitors often have more expensive taste than their pocketbook accommodates).

So, how do you 1) acquire this conversational familiarity with the immediate (and alternative) neighborhoods, and 2) casually and confidently demonstrate your expertise?

Acquiring and Communicating Your Expertise

As we discussed in an earlier chapter, the best way to learn a neighborhood is to be out in it. To know the inventory because you've seen it, smelled it, touched it. There's a big difference between the knowledge you'll gain by physically seeing, smelling and touching the inventory versus simply studying the facts and figures of the inventory on your MLS. Yes, even though most MLS's now offer the ability to (or even require the agent to) include interior and exterior photographs in the listing, nothing beats getting face to face, so to speak, with the real estate in your market.

As a real estate agent, you should always be striving to learn more about your market. And when you do open houses, this gives you a fantastic "excuse" to learn more about a certain segment of it!

Once you've acquired some expertise, it's pretty easy to communicate that expertise to an open house visitor.

First, you have to get the conversational ball rolling. How can you do that with each person who walks in the door?

Frankly, I don't. Try to converse with every visitor, that is. In fact, when I do an open house, I'm happy if I come away with one or two people to follow-up with, even if I had far more visitors than that. If I don't get a comfortable vibe from someone when he walks in the door, I trust that feeling and just let him go. I'll pleasantly answer his questions and offer my opinions if asked, but I'm happy to let him leave without getting his contact information.

But when someone does strike me as a person I might have something in common with, here are a few conversational openers that work well for me.

1. "Have you seen many open houses today?"
2. "Do you live in the neighborhood?"
3. "Have you seen a lot of houses?" (if she indicates she is actively house-shopping)
4. "Who is your agent?" (Note, I don't ask IF she has an agent; I ask WHO her agent is. I find this enormously effective in a) getting a truthful answer and b) getting her to let down her guard with me).

Pretty simple stuff. But most conversation is!

Oh, here's another opening line. My friend Heather asks, "*Have we met? You look familiar.*" She admits that it's a bit sneaky, but swears that it's a fail-safe method for starting up a conversation. Because she works in the same town where she grew up, it's entirely possible she has met this person before, but even if she hasn't, it's a great ice-breaker as they try to figure out if (and how) they (might) know each other. She also says it seems to inspire her visitors to be nicer to her, just in case they actually do know each other, or have friends in common!

Demonstrating your market expertise is best accomplished (with those with whom you have rapport) by simply talking about other houses and neighborhoods that compare favorably with the one you're holding the open house in. Casually, without any hidden agenda; just as a professional real estate agent who knows the market and enjoys talking about it. If, as Melody did with me, you can offer up a few other homes or neighborhoods that might work for the visitor (without sounding hopeful, pushy or desperate!), they might just decide you're The One for them!

Asking for Contact Information

So, at the end of the (open house) day, *should* you ask for contact information?

I don't believe you should ask for it. Crazy, I know, but if you've shifted your paradigm, if you've done a good job preparing for your open house and if you choose your targets wisely, you'll be pleasantly surprised to find that many visitors will initiate further contact with you. Either they'll offer up their contact information voluntarily or they'll ask for yours.

If this isn't happening, it's not because you aren't aggressive enough, clever enough or sly enough to coerce those names and numbers and email addresses from your visitors. So if you want to beat yourself up over the "effectiveness" of your open houses, don't go there. Focus instead on how you can better demonstrate to your visitors that you are the guy or gal they're looking for.

Open Houses—Turning Cheese into Soul

Allow me to pontificate for a moment that I believe the first priority of any open-house-giver is to attempt to sell that house. After all, someone owns that house and has hired you, or an associate of yours to care enough about his listing to try to sell it. And no matter what you tell a seller ahead of time, he really does expect the offers to start pouring in at 4:05.

So, just remember that your primary obligation is to the seller, not yourself. Lecture over.

That said, most of us do look at an open house as an opportunity to pick up buyers. Maybe even sellers. So, how can you do that without resorting to Old School Cheese? (That sound kinda gross, doesn't it?)

My best advice for figuring out what NOT to do is to spend a sunny Sunday visiting other agents' open houses. Egads, some of us are cheesy. Or, if not cheesy, just plain dumb, *aka*, unprepared. I visited an open house last winter and eavesdropped in as a visitor asked the agent how old the furnace was. The agent smiled brightly and said those magic words: "I don't know, but I'd be happy to find out for you!" This piqued my curiosity, so I actually went into the basement and, get this, LOOKED at the furnace. It was obviously brand new. I'd think that anyone who had ever seen a furnace could tell that. Of course, that would have meant that the agent would have had to have made that long journey down the stairs to see for herself—and clearly that was too much to ask.

I've also heard rumors of agents requiring ID before allowing visitors into the property. Okay, maybe in a multi-gazillion-dollar home, but your run-of-the-mill listing? Puh-leeeeeeze.

When you hold an open house, pretend that there's a hidden camera watching your every move (who knows?). Don't do anything the seller wouldn't approve of. Don't criticize the house (that guest you're talking to might know the seller and report back, or he might be a seller prospect himself and be less than impressed with your professionalism!), or aggressively direct visitors toward your fancy list of "other properties they might consider instead."

Besides, it's far less cheesy (and more effective) to be able to simply discuss the market conversationally, rather than push a pre-prepared package on guests.

"There are no traffic jams along the extra mile."
—Roger Staubach

Writing for Dollars, Part I: Staying in Touch with Your SOI

THEY tell us…if we do nothing else to ensure success in a real estate business but one thing, that one thing would be… what?

Any guesses?

Of course. It's Staying in Touch. In touch with our friends. Our family. Our past clients. Our past prospects. Our current clients. Our current prospects. Anyone whose mailing or email address is in our contact manager should be stayed-in-touch-with.

And to hear some talk, that's all it takes to be successful as a real estate agent! Just ensure that your name, number and smiling face are in front of everyone you know on a regular basis and business will pour in.

Ahhhhh, if only it were that simple.

Yes, staying in touch should be a part of your prospecting plan. Absolutely it should. Because "they're" right, if someone forgets you exist or can't find your phone number, they won't go out of their way to remedy that. It IS up to you to make sure neither of these catastrophes happens on your watch.

But I'll tell you a secret. Call me cynical, but I believe there's been a tremendous amount of brainwashing on the subject in our industry, and that the brainwashing was started mostly by companies who want to sell you their stuff to help you stay in touch. And obviously, the more stuff you buy, the more stuff they sell, so they provide all sorts of official-sounding data and statistics to persuade you that you need to stay in touch really really often.

Like I said, call me cynical.

But, I do believe staying in touch is appropriate, effective and necessary. So, let's see how we can "soulfully" stay in touch without driving our friends crazy or spending a fortune.

Why Stay in Touch?

First, it's important to understand—to really understand and internalize—why you are staying in touch with your sphere. If you better understand why you're staying in touch, you'll do a much better job of it—and it'll come more naturally and even be fun.

So, why are you staying in touch? What are you hoping to accomplish?

Well, we don't want to be forgotten, right? That's why we stay in touch?

Eh… sort of.

Keep in mind that there are lots of entities who communicate with us on a regular basis and we don't forget them, but neither do we necessarily look forward to their communications! Your cell phone carrier and utility company who send you a monthly bill or that pesky monthly desk fee bill from your office manager, to name a few.

So, no, the purpose of your staying in touch isn't exactly to simply be remembered. Not exactly.

The purpose of your staying in touch is to be remembered…<u>fondly</u>. To be remembered as someone your audience likes, trusts and would feel comfortable hiring or referring to.

But, the problem with the vast majority of stay-in-touch "programs" is that they aren't really accomplishing that. They're just shoveling your name and number out there on a regular basis without much attention to whether or not what you're providing is enhancing your likeability and credibility among your audience.

And they call it "relationship-building."

How Often Should I Stay in Touch?

I had an interesting conversation recently with my new husband about a real estate transaction he'd had before we met. He mentioned that the agent he used to purchase his first home was a nice guy who had offered to help him find a rental house when he first moved to the area, free of charge. Just helped him. No compensation, no contracts, no obligation. Just helpful help.

So, my husband continued, when it came time to purchase a home, he called up the agent and hired him to be his buyer agent. His point was that because the agent cheerfully gave of his time in the beginning, he ended up with my husband's paying business when he had paying business to give.

I was curious who the agent was and if I knew him or had heard of him…so I asked for the guy's name.

My husband pondered the question. Couldn't come up with a name. John, maybe? He said he'd recognize it if he saw it or heard it, but, darn it, just couldn't remember it right now.

Obviously, my husband hadn't heard from that agent lately. I asked if he'd **ever** heard from the agent after the sale and he didn't think he had. So, I continued the ~~interrogation~~ questioning. I asked if he had heard from the agent, say, two or three times a year for the last five years, would he have been able to recall his name?

He pondered again and said, yes, he would be able to recall the agent's name if he'd heard from him two or three times a year since the sale. But, he said: "*Even once a year would have done it.*"

So, I asked *"What if he'd been in touch every month?"* My husband groaned..."*That would have annoyed me to the point of not wanting to remember him!"*

Which leads to the obvious question: How often do you need to stay in touch with your sphere? How little is too little...how much too much?

The truth is, there isn't one truth. There's no Right Answer that is perfect for everyone. Well, maybe there is, but if so, I don't know what it is. Neither do you, probably. It's a question you'll ask yourself throughout your career and never be fully satisfied with the answer(s) you come up with.

But let's assume my earlier cynicism has merit and that the statistics on the importance of frequently staying in touch tossed out by the personal marketing companies are, um, a bit inflated. Let's pretend that we have no data or statistics to work with; we only have our own intelligence and experience to make the decision as to how often to communicate with our SOI's.

If you can, forget everything you've ever heard about communicating with your SOI and ask yourself...if you were a member of your SOI*, how often would you need to hear from you in order to remember that you sell real estate?

And what sorts of things would:

1) remind you of your existence,
2) inspire you to think of you fondly, and
3) inspire you to call you if and when a real estate need arises?

As we discussed in the first chapter about choosing a prospecting strategy, the best way to evaluate a prospecting strategy is to ask yourself if it would work on you. And prospect accordingly.

But here's an interesting irony.

If what you're sending to your sphere of influence is quality material—and by that I mean that it's of interest to them—then you don't need to worry about being forgotten if they haven't heard from you for two whole weeks. In fact, if

---

* Remember, we're not talking about your geographic farm (see Chapter Eleven); we're talking about people who know you and, presumably, like you, even just a little (if they don't like you, it doesn't matter how often you communicate with them).

you're sending good stuff, you could probably do it just two or three times a year and still see a significant chunk of business as a result.

But the irony is that if your material is interesting and meaningful to your audience, they probably won't mind hearing from you more often! So maybe the punch line is that as long as your stuff is good stuff, you can send it as often (or not) as you like and accomplish your goals either way!

What Should I Write* ABOUT?

You should write about **things of interest to you that will also be of interest to your audience**. You want your writings to be warm and authentic and friendly, so it doesn't make sense to write about things you don't care about or know much about. Take yourself out of the Real Estate Agent persona and put yourself into, say, resident of your city—who happens to sell real estate. Or maybe a dog-owner—who happens to sell real estate. Or a healthy eater—who happens to sell real estate. Or a mother-of-a-toddler—who happens to sell real estate.

In other words, write about things that are meaningful to you and that your audience can relate to. If you can put a real estate agent twist on it, that's fine, but if you can't think of one, that's fine, too.

Speaking of the topics to write about—once you get in the habit, topics will occur to you all the time. I recommend that you keep a list with you to write down topics as they occur to you; before you know it, you'll have enough material for all twelve months!

What Shouldn't I Write About?

I advise against making your communications simply advertisements of your listings. That's a quick way to train your readership to ignore or delete you.

Obviously I don't want you to beg for referrals, or offer bribes for referrals. I don't

---

* Of course, you should also stay in touch with your Group One SOI with more personal and individual activities such as lunch, coffee or margarita dates and one-on-one phone and/or email conversations but this chapter deals specifically with your written communications.

like the idea of asking your SOI for money or sponsorships, regardless of the worthiness of your favorite cause.

I don't recommend doing weekly mortgage updates or focusing too intensely on real estate-specific topics.

I don't think you should tell your audience what a great time to buy it is and apply any sort of pressure on them to Get Moving. There's just no way to do this without sounding pushy. If someone is not in the market to buy real estate, such tactics aren't going to change their minds…and if they are, hopefully they've already been in contact with you about it because they're so impressed with you anyway!

Mass Emails, Newsletters and Postal Mailings

My in-writing SOI stay-in-touch protocol is fairly straightforward. I send out three postal mailings a year and what I call a mass email once a month or so. I don't do newsletters, although I did at one time.

Are you asking what the difference is between a mass email, a postal mailing and a newsletter?

I can help you with that!

- **A mass email** is an email you send to your entire sphere of influence (or segments of it), but the "voice" of the email sounds as if it's written to each person individually. In other words, it has more of a personal email feel than a newsletter or other obviously mass-generated promotional piece.
- **A postal mailing** is a letter, postcard or doo-dad you send to your SOI through the mail.
- **A newsletter**, compared to a mass email, is less personal and more obviously promotional. It might include a variety of articles or topics, and may link to outside websites. It can also be printed and mailed as a postal mailing.

Mass Emails

Mass emails are intended primarily **to start up conversations**. Yes, they'll get your contact information in front of your SOI and will remind them of your existence, but the goal of a mass email is to inspire your audience to respond to you, thus giving you a great opportunity to engage.

I'll give you some ideas on how to do that shortly, but if you look at your mass emails as conversation-starters first and foremost, I think you'll find them easier to write. Especially as you start to see conversations happening—it's incredibly inspiring and motivating. When your mass emails are inspiring your audience to respond to you, you'll actually look forward to doing them. And of course, having conversations—even emailed conversations—can lead to all kinds of wonderful things.

I lived and worked in Denver, so what might I write to my Denver SOI about? Well, once I did a mass email in late March about street-sweeping day (see sidebar) which reminded my friends to walk outside and look at the sign on their street notifying them what day their street would be swept and they'd get a ticket if they parked in the street on that day. Street-sweeping starts in April every year and just about everyone can relate to getting that first ticket of the season.

I love fireworks shows, so I always did an email in July about where the local displays would be. If I listed a particularly interesting property, I might send out a notice of it with a fun description and a virtual tour, although I kept those sorts of things to a minimum—maybe one or two a year.

If you're active in any local activities—maybe the City Council or the PTA or the Booster Club—you can provide information on what they're up to, keeping in mind it needs to be interesting ☺

If your family or a friend owns a trendy local store or restaurant, for example, that might be a good topic to write about or provide a gift certificate for.

Every once in a while, I'll send out what I call a YAY-ME email to my SOI if I've had a particularly note-worthy event in my career—for example, in 2010 I was named among Inman's Most Influential People in Real Estate, so I figured my SOI might be proud of me. I also did a YAY-ME when my book was featured in REALTOR® Magazine. You don't want to YAY-ME all the time, but every once in a while is fine.

Dear Friends,

If you live in Denver, there's a rite of spring that eventually gets all of us.

Beginning in April and running through November, Denver dwellers must be aware of where they park their car on that one special day every month when the street sweepers come through. If your car is in The Zone (that is, on the wrong side of the street on your special day), there's no question you'll get a ticket. Not fun! Oh, I'm not saying that street-sweeping is a bad thing—I'm as happy as anyone to have a clean street—but yes, I do get annoyed (mostly with myself) when I forget and find myself paying that $25 penalty.

So, if you haven't already done so, step outside and remind yourself of Your Special Day. I'm going to go do that right now. I think I'm the third Wednesday...

On a different topic, check out this Highlands/Sunnyside house that just went on the market today. It's a rare combination of vintage charm, 21st century updates & an excellent price! If you love natural woodwork, and also need a "real" house (that is, one with lots of space for your family, furniture & toys), check it out. It's gorgeous!

Hope you're having a good spring, my friends!

Ensuring Your Mass Emails Get Opened

Here are a few tips to ensure that your readers actually open your mass emails—and then we'll move on to talk a little about newsletters and postal mailings.

- **Tip #1: Don't try to make your mass emails works of art**
  The simpler, the better. You don't need a fancy banner and you don't need a 3-column newsletter design. In fact, the simpler the email is, the more likely it will be read and, even more importantly, the more likely it will be responded to. If someone responds to your email, you can start up a conversation with him that could lead to wonderful things. But people rarely respond to fancy eNewsletters because they feel impersonal. Impressive, perhaps, but impersonal.

  I'd much rather see you use your custom email signature at the bottom of the email rather than a big splashy banner at the top. And as more and more people work from smart phones—these banners are harder to get past when you open the email in the device.

  So, don't agonize over making your emails works of art.

- **Tip #2: Related to Tip #1—Less is More**
  Your mass email should only cover one topic. Again, you are not trying to blow away your audience with your knowledge of everything under the sun—your goal is to remind them of your existence, inspire them to think of you fondly, and hopefully start up a conversation. You can do that in a couple of paragraphs. All the rest is distracting fluff.

- **Tip #3: Don't make people click on a link or open an attachment to get to the meat of your note**
  Put whatever it is you're saying IN the email itself. When you link or attach, you've added an unnecessary hurdle for your readers to jump over to experience whatever wonderfulness you're sending them.

  For example, I have a lender friend who sends me a Mortgage Update every Sunday. The cover page simply says "Here is your weekly mortgage update from Jon Smith." Then I'm supposed to open the attachment to see a boilerplate spreadsheet that is, unfortunately, of no earthly interest to me. So, I'll let you guess how many times I've clicked on that attachment after the first time.

On the other hand, I have another lender friend who writes every other Friday or so with a quick, friendly and clever commentary on the mortgage world. He writes it in his own voice and always makes me smile. And I almost always respond to him and start up a little conversation. Guess which lender is my go-to guy in Denver?

Newsletters (printed and emailed)

I see a lot of newsletters coming through the mail or inbox. Some are...well, let's just say that some are better than others. Most are clearly purchased "as is" and distributed at the touch of a button (or click of a mouse). Some display a little bit of customization, such as a spot to write a "personal" note or feature a listing or two. A few appear to be 100% created from scratch.

What are the typical topics covered in a real estate agent's newsletter? Lessee... home improvement tips, gardening ideas, recipes, market stats, Just Listed and Just Sold announcements, mortgage news...sorry...but YAWWWWWWWN. Not only does every real estate newsletter seem to follow the same pattern, but half the time, the information is so boilerplate as to not even apply to the local market!

So let's step back a bit.

What's the Real Purpose of Your Newsletter?

Is it to...

- educate your audience on the average Days on Market or Price per Square Foot in your area?
- impress the reader by displaying your new listings or bragging about your recent closings?
- ensure your friends know how important it is to winterize their sprinkler systems?
- share your gardening expertise?

If you answered "yes" to any of the above, I'll encourage you to re-read the first part of this chapter and think about your answer.

Isn't the ultimate goal of a newsletter simply to inspire your audience to like you and remember you?

We can debate all day about what exactly "like" means but, in general, by sending a newsletter, you're hoping that the person who receives it thinks a little more highly of you than they did before it was sent. Which naturally leads to them being just a little more likely to remember you (fondly) than they were the day before.

So, what, in a newsletter, might inspire that reaction? Or conversely, what might be the kiss of death?

Inspiring a newsletter recipient to smile is best accomplished **not** with gardening tips, Just Sold notices or descriptions of your listings, but rather with interesting content that reflects YOU—your voice, your personality. And the best way to do that is to write the content yourself.

Now, don't panic. Writing interesting content yourself is not all that hard, especially if you work under the principle that less is more. Don't feel your newsletter has to be formally formatted with a Volume Number, Table of Contents and a three-column layout. Nope. In fact, a simple email or letter-style newsletter may work much better. No sidebars, graphics or sales-pitches required.

Professionally designed newsletters may be impressive but, frankly, they're a dime a dozen these days. Many readers will assume that the fancy newsletter is either boilerplate or sales-pitchy, and, if pressed for time, are likely to hit DELETE (or toss it in the trash) without reading it. (However, if you're going to include fancy graphics or custom designs, please please, please ensure that it's done well. Amateur-ish newsletters send the wrong message to your audience!)

Make sure your newsletter goes out from YOU—as in, from Your Name. Not from some professional-sounding company or even your fancy tagline. YOUR NAME. Period. If your readers don't immediately recognize the sender, again, they're likely to hit DELETE (or toss it) before investigating further.

Better than Nothing?

Okay, Jennifer, I agree in principle but I don't want to/have time to/have the skill to/ have the patience to create my own content. Isn't it Better than Nothing to at least send SOMETHING?

Nice try, but no. It's not. Especially when you're sending out that SOMETHING to your Sphere of Influence—*aka* your friends and acquaintances. If you must, go ahead and send out SOMETHING (defined here as a cheesy, dorky, boilerplate yawn-er) to strangers, but please don't do it to your sphere.

Why?

Your sphere of influence contact database is precious and should be treated as such. In fact, it may be the most valuable tool in your prospecting arsenal for getting good business and bringing in juicy paychecks. Treat it with the respect it deserves. Let me rephrase that. Treat the people who make up your contact database with the respect they deserve.

As I've mentioned once or twice, every single person in your sphere of influence has the potential to bring a $10,000 check your way. More than one, even. That's a fact. So, it's well worth the effort to MAKE an effort to inspire those special people to smile and think fondly of you every time they hear from you. Don't do anything that sends a message that the person is simply a name on your list, someone worthy of your prospecting efforts, but not your personal attention. And that's exactly what canned, boilerplate, cheesy marketing material does. It sends the message that the recipient is just a name on your list.

Frankly, I'd rather take the chance that my sphere of influence forgets I sell real estate rather than take the chance that they roll their eyes every time they hear from me. If I'm not willing to take the time to create interesting, relevant, non-cheesy promotional material to send to my precious sphere of influence, then a sphere of influence business model may not be the right model for me.

Postal Mailings

My postal mailings are done primarily to physically get my business card or whatever my doo-dad of the year is in my SOI's hands so that they have my contact information.

I do two or three a year. That's plenty to get my business card out there, it doesn't cost me a fortune and I don't abuse my privilege in someone's mail box.

One postal mailing is always a personal letter that takes the form of an annual family newsletter. What I've been up to, what's new and exciting in my life—stuff like that.

I also usually do a holiday card, usually with a little doo-dad. One year I did Denver Sushi Bar magnets and the year before I sent out my Referral Directory magnet. I used to do full-size calendars this time of year.

Then I'll do one other mailing, if I can think of something I'm excited about. I can live with this third mailing being something more boilerplate or non-custom, as long as it's of value, not cheesy, and represents who I am.

If you will be addressing your envelopes, follow these Four Golden Rules of Envelope-Addressing.

1. Hand-write the envelopes. It won't take that long. Just do it.
2. Make sure for sure for sure that you spell the addressee's name right.
3. Don't use your corporate or franchise's logo'd envelopes.
4. Always use a real stamp. No postage meters.

The Technology of Staying in Touch

Let's talk a little about the technology of mass emails and eNewsletters.

I hesitate to name names here in a book that will hopefully be around for a few years, which could render my recommendations useless or worse, erroneous. So, I'll keep this as generic as possible, and if you want to know more about which technologies I'm currently using, just ask me.

For mass emailing, I currently use a popular online newsletter program. It's not perfect, but until I find something that is, I'll continue using it. If your SOI email list isn't very big, you might be able to use your regular email system—such as Outlook or your online webmail interface—but you need to fully understand the risks of being identified as a spammer by your audience's servers. It happened to me on my Comcast email address and for a few weeks I couldn't email anyone who also had a Comcast email address.

Many contact management systems offer an online newsletter feature, although I wonder if they do it as well as a company that specializes in sending online newsletters as their primary service.

The biggest unresolved dilemma I've found with using specialized service providers to create and send out mass emails is that the more flexible ones (that is, the ones that allow you to add subscribers without getting their explicit permission) tend to be blocked by the more aggressive spam filters. But the trade-off is, obviously, that you CAN add people without making them jump through hoops, and it's easy enough for them to opt out. Many less-flexible online newsletter programs require that the person opt-in or confirm their desire to be there on your list, which will dramatically cut down on the number of names you end up with. Not because they don't want to hear from you, necessarily, but because they simply didn't take that last step to confirm their subscription. However, these systems tend to have better delivery rates.

Doo-Dad unto Others...

Ahhhh... where would we real estate agents be without our doo-dads? Or maybe I should ask, where would the doo-dad companies be without us real estate agents?

Sorry, that's the cynical side of me peeking out again.

What's a doo-dad? A doo-dad is a promotional gift, trinket or gizmo-gadget we buy in bulk to send out to our spheres of influence in hopes of reminding them we exist. And of course, we hope that, as they're remembering we exist, they're also racking their brains to think of someone to refer to us because they're so darned impressed with that doo-dad we sent them.

Popular doo-dads include calendars, pens, scratch-pads, reusable grocery bags, magnets, squooshy stress balls, seed packets and the like. Doo-dads typically are customized with the agent's name, number and smiling face, and often with that oh-so-adorable "I HEART Referrals!" slogo!

Especially for Introverts—The Real Estate Numbers Game in Reverse—Did You Impress More than You Annoyed?

As the Introverted Real Estate Agent's New Best Friend (I just made that up), I give out a lot of advice on how to make a real estate career work even if you aren't the most outgoing, charismatic social butterfly in town. The other day I was asked about the appropriateness of adding people to your mailing list (either email or snail-mail) without their permission. Spam issues aside (we're talking about people we know, not strangers), many introverts are hesitant to begin any structured written communication with a friend or acquaintance for fear of annoying them.

I get that. Oh, how I get that. I agonize over my mailing list every time I send something out, whether it's to my real estate sphere of influence or my Sell with Soul readership. I wonder if I'm communicating too much; if I'm wearing out my welcome; or conversely, if I'm not communicating enough and my audience has forgotten who I am. I worry about the appropriateness of including a little promo for my next product or new listing. Conversely, I worry that if I don't, I'm not fulfilling my duty to myself to effectively market my stuff.

It's easy to over-think such things and end up doing nothing. Which is a bad plan. So, if this sounds anything like you, here are a few thoughts to put your mind at ease...

First, ask yourself if what you're getting ready to send out is something you're proud of. If it's something you'd enjoy receiving in your mailbox or inbox. Or, egads, if it's some cheesy newsletter or sales piece that you'd toss without reading if it were sent to you.

If your communication is something you are proud of and would enjoy receiving, then move on down to the next point. If it's not, if you're actually embarrassed by your effort, then you need to honor that gut feeling and return to the drawing board. Because sending something cheesy or dorky is NOT better than doing nothing at all!

If you're pleased with your piece, send it out. To everyone. Here's the thing. A few might be annoyed or feel spammed. That's a fact. But most won't. The vast majority won't. If you're sending out good stuff, most will enjoy it and be impressed by you. Which is good for business.

Nah, seriously, I like doo-dads in moderation. While I disagree with the philosophy that a steady stream of doo-dads qualifies as "relationship-building," I think a well-designed, well-timed and well-placed doo-dad functions quite nicely as a reminder of an agent's existence and professionalism.

Of course, the opposite is true as well. Doo-dads that are poorly designed, poorly executed or poorly chosen function quite nicely as, yes, a reminder of an agent's existence but certainly not of his or her professionalism.

Frankly, I'd rather someone forget me than think me unprofessional, and some of the doo-dads promoted by doo-dad distributors are, well, eye-rolling ridiculously unprofessional.

Cool Doo-Dads versus Not-Cool Doo-Dads

So, what makes a doo-dad "cool" as opposed to "not-cool"?

Well, in my opinion, there are three categories of doo-dads:

1. Cheesy, silly doo-dads,
2. Ho-hum, predictable doo-dads, and
3. Soulful doo-dads.

Category One—the Cheesy, Silly Doo-Dad

Fly-swatters and pot-holders come to mind in this category. I'd also put a lot of other promotional items in here—doo-dads that aren't at all related to real estate and/or don't represent you as a professional. I almost hate to give any more examples because I'll likely offend many of my readers who have purchased and sent out these doo-dads in the past (or are planning to next week)! But this category includes your basic junk that makes the recipient roll his eyes and think the doo-dad-giver is an idiot.

Category Two—the Ho-hum, Predictable Doo-Dad

The second category is where most real estate agents' efforts lie. Promotional trinkets that are harmless but not memorable. They aren't cheesy or silly, but neither are they any different from what every other real estate agent (and financial planner, insurance agent and hair-stylist) does. We've all done them, myself included, and it's not likely they've damaged our reputations or credibility.

I consider generic calendars, sports schedules, pens, scratch pads—anything boilerplate or familiar—to fall into this category, although you can make these items soulful with a little effort.

Again, there's nothing wrong with doo-dads in this category.

Category Three—the Soulful Doo-Dad

But the third category—the soulful doo-dad—that's a whole different story. A soulful doo-dad is a trinket that, well, that you put some thought into. And because you put some thought into it, the people who receive it are much more likely to smile, think of you fondly and hold onto your doo-dad. In other words… it's special. And it makes the person who receives it feel a little special.

Is creating a soulful doo-dad more work than a non-soulful one? Yep. Absolutely. And it might even cost a little more! But again, if you're going to spend the money and time creating and sending out a doo-dad, doesn't it make sense to make it special, even if that takes a little extra work and a few more dollars?

Gimme an Example of a Soulful Doo-Dad, Please

Well, anything you created yourself probably qualifies. As we discussed earlier in this chapter, the more YOU that goes into a promotional piece, the more effective it's likely to be. Now don't fret, when I say you created it yourself, I don't mean that you designed and printed it out on your fancy all-in-one printer; I mean that you came up with the idea and/or used your own words or content.

The House of Magnets (www.houseofmagnets.com) offers a great example of a create-it-yourself magnet—The Top Ten created by none other than yours truly! It's a completely customizable list of the Top Ten Whatevers in your town, city or market area—and you choose the Top Ten! I did Denver's Top Ten Sushi Bars, my friend Susan did her Top Ten Dessert Spots in Old Town Alexandria and my friend Debbie did a Top Ten Day Trips in her area.

But that's just one example of a soulful doo-dad.

Some agents have taken the ho-hum recipe card concept and made it soulful by sending out their own personal recipes. While this may not suit some personalities, it's perfectly appropriate for others. I've known agents to use local schoolchildren's artwork to create a calendar or decorative magnet. One agent I know who owns her real estate company printed her distinctive logo on reusable grocery bags. That same agent sends out monthly postcards with a different picture of her (adorable) son with a clever call-to-action in a cartoon speech bubble over his head.

So, Jennifer, Is "This" Soulful?

After I've done a blog or newsletter or teleseminar show about doo-dads, I always get a flood of emails from agents who want to know if their idea for a doo-dad qualifies as "soulful."

And, being the ~~opinionated~~ helpful soul I am, I try to answer them definitively. I explain why this doo-dad IS soulful and why that doo-dad is NOT and back up my opinion with detailed explanations. But finally, one guy called me on it. He asked me why I thought a reusable grocery bag was cool, while a meat thermometer was not cool. Neither related to real estate, neither was particularly clever and both were equally useful.

Hmmmmm. I was stumped. He was right. There really was no discernible difference between the two items; one simply appealed to me and the other one didn't.

The agent persisted—"*Jennifer, what's the difference? Why do you like one, but not the other?*"

After stumbling around searching for just the right response to clear things up for him, I came up with this little piece of brilliance:

"*I dunno. I just do.*"

And that answer might actually be good enough. It comes back down to the Golden Rule—to paraphrase:

"Doo-Dad unto others as you would like to be Doo-Dad'ed unto!"

We can't possibly know for sure what our spheres of influence would find useful or valuable. So, perhaps the best we can do is to ask ourselves what we would like, what we would appreciate and what we would keep.

And Doo-Dad (or not) accordingly...

One Last Thought About Doo-Dads...

Don't "burden" your sphere of influence with your doo-dads.

What do I mean by "burden"?

Well, think about when you receive a doo-dad from a stranger, you have no qualms tossing it into the trash if you don't want it. No muss, no fuss, no angst—doo-dad gone and forgotten.

But when you get a doo-dad you don't really want from someone you know, you aren't so quick to throw it away. You might hold onto it for a while, out of respect for that relationship.

Um, yeah, Jennifer—that's the point! I want the recipient of my fancy doo-dad to hold onto it—DUH!

Not so fast. Let's think about what's going through the doo-dad recipient's mind. This person really doesn't want to keep that doo-dad. It's likely just one more thing to find a home for and to collect dust. But his loyalty to you forces him to make a decision that he's going to be uncomfortable with either way. Throw it away and feel guilty or don't throw it away and feel irritated.

That's what I mean by "burden." I don't want my precious SOI spending one second trying to decide whether or not they're willing to hurt my feelings by throwing away that trinket I sent. And I REALLY don't want them to make the decision to throw it away, thus subconsciously relegating me and my service to the round file. *<shudder>*

Let me give you an example. Every year, a particular doo-dad seems to make the rounds in early July. It's a little American flag on a stick that serves no real purpose except to give the real estate agent an excuse to drop it off. There really isn't anything the recipient can do with the flag except maybe put it in his pencil holder.

This is the epitome of a burdensome doo-dad. First, no one wants to throw away an American flag, especially at such a patriotic time of year! And of course, since it comes from a friend, that adds even more fuel to that I-Feel-Guilty fire, should the recipient choose to dispose of it.

So, don't doo-dad for the sheer sake of doo-dad'ing. If you wouldn't appreciate receiving it, don't assume anyone else will, either.

"Writing comes more easily if you have something to say."
Sholem Asch

CHAPTER TEN

Writing for Dollars, Part II:
Blogging for Business

BLOGGING, like social media, is a form of self-promotion that its proponents claim you *must do* if you're to survive in today's real estate market. On the other hand, the nay-sayers claim that blogging is already passé, and if you haven't already started to blog, there's no real sense in it at this late date.

I won't enter into the debate, other than to say a few words (I can't help myself, I guess)…

Do I think it's necessary to blog to survive? Absolutely not. Just as you don't have to cold-call, door-knock, mass-mail, Twitter or Link-In. Blogging is simply another avenue to build your business; if it's right for you, it'll work for you. If it's not right for you, feel free to leave it completely out of your business model.

However, I suspect that those who say blogging has passed its prime may have some valid arguments. Specifically that the blogosphere is flooded with canned, pitchy and poorly written material to the point that the intended reader throws up his hands in frustration. Others claim that the more "immediate" or abbreviated forms of online conversation are preferred over the passive and more lengthy nature of a blog, even a well-written one. And, truthfully, it's tough to keep up a blog, especially if you haven't yet built an audience for your words to provide a consistent source of reward and reinforcement for your efforts.

The proponents of blogging, however, are just as prolific in their praise. But before we decide whether or not blogging is a viable source of business for *you*, let's back up a minute. What is a blog, where is a blog, how do you blog, why do you blog and who do you blog for?

To answer these burning questions, I've invited my friend Bob Stewart, Chief Evangelist at ActiveRain (www.ActiveRain.com - only the greatest real estate blogging platform on the planet!) to share his brilliance with y'all!

Bob Stewart Sez...

I must admit, the first time I ever heard the term "blog," it conjured up images of a space alien in a Star Wars movie. I was certain that "Blog" was destined to take over the planet Bothawui and save the Martyrs Constellation from extinction at the hands of Darth Vader.

My imagination had gotten the best of me, of course. "Blog" is little more than an abridgment of the terms "web" and "log." A "web log" or online diary consisting of words, pictures, videos and links to other blogs and web pages generally focused on a particular theme or topic. While most blogs consist primarily of text, the "vlog," or video blog is becoming increasingly popular as video becomes a more accepted medium on the net. The blog platform Posterous.com has made the image blog very popular as it has become easier to take pictures with a camera phone and upload the images to the web immediately.

Jennifer's Blog at ActiveRain:
www.activerain.com/blogs/sellwithsoul

Blogging as the Foundation of Your Social Media Strategy

A successful social media* strategy should contain your blog as the anchor. There is only so much information that one can convey in a Facebook status update

---

* we talk more about social media in Chapter Thirteen

or 140-character update on Twitter. The local information that your consumers crave takes much more than 140 characters. Social media platforms like Facebook and Twitter afford you the opportunity to disseminate your message to your followers like never before, but often that message can't be summed up in a neat little package.

Explaining the loan application process, informing buyers of the importance of the inspection process or detailing the nuances of living in a particular neighborhood would take hundreds of "tweets" or status updates. Having this information in one good blog post is the key to providing this information to those who are seeking it.

The power of social media sites like Facebook and Twitter is the coalescing nature of the content absorbed. Taken on its own, any one tweet or any one status update may seem irrelevant or mundane, but it's the sum of a person's tweets or the sum of his status updates that gives you a better sense of who the person is and allows you to connect with him as a human being. Your blog works in a similar fashion, but each post taken on its own will in no way be mundane or irrelevant. Instead, each post has the potential to inform and educate past clients, potential clients and those who seek the information you are providing. And the totality of your blog will give consumers a clear and concise picture of how you do business.

ActiveRain member and super-blogger Broker Bryant Tutas of Poinciana, Florida shares that, *"I no longer have to educate my clients about the way I do business when I first meet with them. Many of them have been following my blog for weeks or months before ever contacting me and have a unique understanding of the way I operate."*

It's this kind of positioning that has clients seeking out the services of Broker Bryant to request that he be the person to list their home—instead of the more traditional way in which sellers have selected agents in the past: by interviewing multiple agents and picking the one they feel the most comfortable with. Broker Bryant's clients already feel comfortable with him, having obtained insight into how he operates his business through his blog. They are never startled by his pricing methods or what he asks his sellers to do prior to listing a home because they have already read about it in his blog.

"I started writing my blog because I was a solo agent," says Bryant Tutas. "My wife and I had a small brokerage and we didn't come into contact every day with other agents, as you would if you were in a big brokerage office. It was an outlet for me to share ideas, get feedback and hopefully educate some of my peers along the way."

The first time a family contacted him as a result of his blog it suddenly made sense that they would find the information he was sharing relevant and important to their goals of trying to sell their home. *"I was writing about the things I do in my real estate business, things that sellers appreciate when they want to sell their home. But I wasn't doing it at first to attract clients."* He was doing it for the reasons he mentioned before, to share and engage with other real estate agents.

The Neighborhood Expert

The real estate agent as a local neighborhood expert has long been the goal of agent marketing campaigns. Agents have been farming neighborhoods since Americans first starting congregating in subdivisions post-World War Two. Since that time, real estate agents have been trying to convince sellers and buyers that it is they who have the most intimate knowledge of their neighborhood and, therefore, are the most qualified agent to sell their home. How have agents historically convinced neighbors of this local prowess?

Saturation is how. Agents saturated their target neighborhood with as much advertising as they could afford. Of course, that advertising—television, radio, print, landscape—all had a finite amount of space. There is only so much time on television or radio. There are only so many bus benches or billboards. There are only so many newspapers and magazines. At some point the local mail man became our mule and began stuffing our neighbors' mailboxes with postcards, but we only had so much money to send them and the mail box is only so big. So it became the person who could provide the most saturation who got top billing in the minds of neighbors. "Top saturation" simply meant, "I have the most money to spend."

But blogging has completely turned this approach on its ear.

A blog gives any agent who is familiar with a certain market or neighborhood the chance to showcase that expertise for the world to see. And since our clients are increasingly heading online to find their next home, we can also assume they are searching for information about what it's like to live in the neighborhoods they're considering.

So, What Can Real Estate Agents Write About to Demonstrate Their Expertise?

- School information
- Subdivision profiles
- Neighborhood architecture
- Tips for buying or selling
- Entertainment options
- Local businesses
- Neighborhood profiles
- Transportation
- Employment opportunities
- Nightlife
- Childcare

Some of this information is sought by the consumer prior to purchasing a home; some of it is sought once they are settled in afterwards. Delivering this information in either instance enhances the brand of the real estate agent as the local expert.

A Few Words from Jennifer—What Do You Blog About?

Truthfully, just about anything you observe or that happens to you in your daily life is potential fodder for a great blog. And once you start blogging, you'll find inspiration everywhere. It's the curse of the obsessive blogger—the inability to shut off that blogging voice in your head that's always composing your next blog. I recommend that agents carry around a little notebook or scratch pad to record their ideas for blogs as they go about their business day; you'll be surprised how many topics occur to you once you've been blogging a little while.

But back to what to blog about...well, think about topics your ideal buyer or seller might search for online. Because, keep in mind, your potential clients aren't going online looking for a real estate blogger; they're online to get information about the real estate market you serve. Even if they aren't specifically looking for a real estate agent right now, if you show up in searches and appear to have your finger on the pulse of the area, they might, just might, remember you and return when they're ready for someone just like you!

Keep in mind that you don't have to blog about all real estate, all of the time. Someone who is searching online for their next home is also likely searching for information about the area. So if you show up as someone who knows a little something about the local shopping, the parks, the hot potato political issues, the area's history, the schools, the commercial development and the restaurants, you'll come across as an even more credible area expert.

Bob Continues...

Virginia Hepp, a real estate agent in Mesquite, Nevada credits her blog with literally saving her career. In a market that had slowed to a snail's pace, Hepp, who worked mostly from referrals, had almost no online presence, and her blog became her savior. "*I found that I had more time on my hands than I had ever had before,*" she says. "*When I found ActiveRain and I saw other agents around the country writing about their local markets, and then bragging about the fantastic placement they were getting on the search engines, a light bulb went off for me.*"

Hepp set out to canvass her market using her blog. She began writing posts about everything she could think of; she became a roving reporter of sorts. Every interaction, every grand opening, every community event would become potential fodder for her blog.

"*There is no absolute way to have a successful real estate blog,*" says Brad Andersohn, Community Manager with ActiveRain. "*What works for one person may not work at all for another person. Some people are comfortable sharing things about their family and more personal details about themselves. Others stick strictly with the traditional topics a real estate agent would know; market reports, listings, marketing strategies.*"

Even though Andersohn has seen agents succeed with a dry, professional approach, he believes that adding your own personality to your blog is important in the long run. "*Maintaining a blog is hard work. There are days when you might not be able to think of anything to write and you just don't want to do it. When your blog is full of your personality it's easier to get through those days. Your readers will not be surprised if you head outside of real estate and talk about your disappointment with your favorite football team or the great set your band played the night before.*

"After 20 years in customer service, I really believe that people want to work with someone they like and someone they can trust," concludes Andersohn. We could surmise then that including personal elements in your blog allows the reader to get a better sense of who you are as a person, whether they would like working with you and if they would trust you.

A Few Words from Jennifer—Conversational versus Informational

An effective blog can be made up of "conversational" and "informational" posts. By "conversational," I mean that you let your personality shine through in your blog. If a reader stumbles onto your blog and reads a few posts, he'll feel as if he knows you already, which builds loyalty. Many bloggers report that their new clients tell them they'd been reading their blogs for months or even years before making contact.

By "informational" I'm referring to posts about your local market and/or individual listings. These are the blogs that tend to show up in searches, particularly the market-related ones.

Back to Bob...

How to Write a Blog Post

Here are the three primary components of a blog post: the title, the body of the post—also known as the content—and the tags, or the way to organize the posts.

Let's start with the title. The title is important for two reasons. It tells your reader what they are about to read and it serves as an important component in getting your post to rank well in the search engines.

People who are online often have short attention spans. Search engines have spoiled us to expect exactly what we want exactly when we want it. If we land on a page and we are expecting one thing, only to actually be shown something else, most of us are off that within seconds. So your title is important because it tells your reader what they are about to read. It needs to be informative in that it accurately explains the content below it, and be enticing so the reader actually chooses to read the content.

The search engine component of the title is harder to understand but exponentially more important. The title of your blog post should become the URL, or web address, of the post. On the ActiveRain Real Estate Network, this is done automatically for you. On other platforms like Wordpress or Blogger you can set your blog up to act in this fashion. Search engines look at the URL in determining how to rank certain pieces of content. It's only one factor, but having a URL that matches a certain keyword phrase can help get your blog posts to rank well in search results.

In addition, the title of your post can be set up to become the title of your page. Every page on the Internet has the ability to be given a title. The title of the page explains to the search engines what the page is about. If the title of the blog post becomes the title of the page as well as the URL of the page, it becomes very easy for the search engine to understand what the page is about.

One of the keys to writing good titles for real estate posts is to use geographic terms in the title. While you may very well be interested in targeting someone looking for information about "getting my home ready to sell," you probably don't want or need to attract everyone across the country who is searching for that topic!

Of course you could argue that if the content were that good the non-local consumer might contact you anyway for a referral to their area, but that's not going to happen. Instead, if we are an agent in Seattle, we want to make sure that we use our geographic terms in our titles, so we target consumers in Seattle looking for the information we provide. Therefore, that same article will be more effective if we title it "Getting my Seattle Home Ready to Sell."

The second component of the blog post is the body, or content, of the post. The part where you actually deliver that unique knowledge that makes you the local expert. We won't talk about exactly what to write here; hopefully you pick that up throughout this section. However, we will talk about some good rules for getting the most out of your content with the search engines.

Strive to make your articles between 300 and 500 words. Any shorter than that and you may not be delivering valuable information (not always of course, but it's a good rule of thumb). If your article is longer than that, you may want to break it into two parts and run them in two blogs.

Your article should be focused on one topic and geared toward ranking for a certain keyword phase or term. That keyword phrase should be in your title and it should also be repeated in the body of your post 2% to 4% of the time. This means that if you have 300 words in your post, you want the keyword phrase to be repeated 6 to 12 times. This is called keyword density. A recommended keyword density of 2% to 4% has been shown to be optimal. Of course, nobody knows exactly what Google or the other search engines are looking for, but based on years of optimizing pages to rank well, we believe this to be an acceptable range that will keep your pages from getting penalized.

"Penalized?"

If you've spent any amount of time studying search engine optimization you've come across the phrase "keyword stuffing." Exceeding 4% keyword density will start to make your posts look fishy and the last thing we want is for Google to consider us fishy.

The last component of a blog post is the "tag" or "category." This is the primary way to organize different posts so they are easy for a visitor to find. Since blogs are usually displayed in chronological order, with the most recent post at the top of the page and older posts lower down or on subsequent pages, it's important to provide a way for readers to find older posts. This is where tags or categories come into play.

Let's say that you write a post about getting pre-approved for a FHA loan. It may have two tags, "FHA Loan" and "Getting Pre-Approved." Your blog would then incorporate both of these tags and create a new page out of both tags. Someone looking for information about "FHA Loan" could find your post about getting pre-approved on that tag page possibly along with other posts about the FHA loan process. Similarly, if they were to go to the "Getting Pre-Approved" tag, they would find your post about getting an FHA pre-approval along with other posts you may have written about "Getting pre-approved" for other types of loans, not just FHA.

Many bloggers overdo their tagging to the point it becomes a hindrance to use their tags to search for content. As you start to blog, keep in mind that your tags are a great way to group similar information together, so make a concerted effort to ensure that your tags are clean and easy to understand. Try to avoid simple duplications such as using a singular word one time and plural version of the word the next time. "Home Improvement" and "Home Improvements" are most likely the exact same topic, yet creating both tags creates extra places on your blog for your content to be housed. Stay consistent and your readers will be able to navigate your content much more easily.

Writing blog posts that rank well in the search engines is not rocket science, even though you probably get phone calls every week assuring you it's impossible for you to optimize your site ranking on your own and offering you their service for a breath-taking amount of money. But it's not true. Just one well-written blog can immediately begin to rank on the first page of Google for its topic, some-times within 24 hours.

And Now Back to Jennifer…

Your Blog "Voice"

The general consensus on successful blogging is to blog in your own voice. The more authentic and transparent you are in your blogging, the more likely you are to attract like-minded followers, or heck, any followers at all, like-minded or not! If you write in a predictable, boilerplate, corporate tone, you'll lose the interest of anyone who stumbles across your blog. Conversely, if your writing style is more along the lines of how you speak in normal conversation, your audience will feel as if they know you and, if what you say is relevant to them at the time, they'll be far more inclined to learn more about you.

Of course, you'll want to remember that once something is online, it's forever, so temper your authenticity and transparency with a dose of good sense. Don't pepper your blogs with four-letter words or discuss intimate issues that have no business being in the public domain. Proofread and/or use spell-check to ensure you're coming across as an RCHB. Try not to ramble; in a blog, less is almost always more. The famous blogger ☺ Mark Twain once said, "If I'd had more time, I'd have written less."

Is Blogging Right for You?

As with any other prospecting method, blogging is right for some... and not at all right for others. If it's right for you, it truly can be a significant source of business for you; many SWS-followers are finding their blog to be their most significant business source, even more productive than their spheres of influence (oh, my!). Others, well, not so much.

It's not hard to determine if blogging is right for you, really. Ask yourself:

- Do I like to write?
- Am I a reasonably good writer?
- Am I a decent speller and do I have a grasp of proper sentence structure?
- Am I reasonably computer-literate?
- Do I enjoy communicating with others online?
- Does the idea of sitting down several mornings (or evenings) a week to write a 300-500-word blog sound like something I'll actually do?
- If I were asked right now to come up with four or five topics to blog about, could I?
- If I were sent out to spend a day in my favorite neighborhood, taking pictures, previewing homes, visiting the parks, shopping in the stores, eating in the restaurants—do I think I would come home with a sweet little list of interesting things I observed to write about?

Some agents simply aren't suited to developing an online persona and that's just fine! I know agents who are delightful in person, but put them in front of a computer (after you've dragged them there kicking and screaming) and all that delightfulness quickly fades. They lose their spark and it's obvious they'd rather be doing anything other than sitting at that keyboard.

Others tend to be far more delightful online (Brad Paisley's song, *I'm So Much Better Online,* comes to mind!) than in person and can happily sit at a keyboard for hours at a time…and have to be dragged **away** kicking and screaming to venture out into the "real" world!

Of course, those are the two extremes and most of us fall somewhere in between. But you probably already know yourself well enough to determine if blogging is something you want to invest your time and energy in…or if that precious time and energy are better focused elsewhere. As with all PWS strategies…trust that feeling.

For the record, I love blogging as a prospecting strategy. It's intelligent. It's interactive. It's 100% attraction-oriented. It provides the opportunity to be authentic and attract a like-minded audience. It provide honest value to others. It's addictive, which makes it a fun and sustainable prospecting activity. It's cheap.

It works.

And it's a perfect example of Prospecting with Soul.

Forums

Another online venue you might consider is participation on local real estate forums hosted by national real estate-specific portals. Today, a good example would be Trulia (www.trulia.com); however, by the time you're reading this, it may be old news. Trulia and sites like it are real estate-related sites for consumers, but they also offer real estate agents opportunities to attract and interact with potential customers via their forums.

One of the fun features of these forums is that consumers can post questions about the market they're interested in, and if you sign up to be notified of the questions (in your market area), you can answer their questions and potentially start up a conversation!

However, take care not to sales-pitch too much in your responses. If you strive to be helpful, informative and friendly in your answers, that'll take you a lot further than simply pushing yourself on the question-asker.

JENNIFER'S BLOG:

How to Keep Your Blog from Being Dorky!

I know you aren't DORKY. I'll bet if I asked a dozen of your friends if you're an interesting, personable, caring, creative kinda guy or gal, they'd confirm that you are. So, why is it that those in our profession insist on creating written promotional material that screams, "I'M BORING AS DIRT AND HAVE ABSOLUTELY NOTHING INTERESTING TO SAY!"?

You know what I'm talking about. The corporate-inspired announcement letters we send to our friends and family when we go into real estate. Our business cards with sappy, meaningless tag lines. Our online profiles that might put the reader to sleep if they actually get past the first paragraph. Where did all that personality go? Where are YOU?

When you blog, don't be DORKY, be YOU. If you're sappy, blog sappy. If you're sarcastic, blog sarcastic. If you're funny, blog funny. If you wake up one morning frustrated as heck about something or other, blog about it. Conversely, if you're tickled pink by a recent encounter at the health food store, write about that. If you have a brilliant aha! moment standing in line at the post office, there's a blog in there somewhere!

(Oh, one caveat. If you're a sloppy writer, don't blog sloppy! Use your spell check, capitalize appropriately and be sure to use your <enter> key on a regular basis.)

Don't try to write about topics you couldn't care less about. Not a political type? Don't try to write about local political issues. Don't know much about the economy? Leave the economic outlook blogs to someone who does. Not into cultural events? Don't bother trying to write intelligently about the new opera in town.

But don't worry too much about speaking to any particular audience. YOU do the talking and the right audience will find you. And you know what? If your blogs come from YOUR voice, you'll stand a much better chance of enjoying the process enough to keep it up.

To summarize, to avoid being a DORKY blogger:

- Write from YOUR voice, that real person who has a terrific personality.

- Write about topics of interest to YOU.

- Proofread, proofread, proofread.

Now, go get 'em, you UNDORKY blogger, you!

Dear Real Estate Professional,
I'd Like to See a House, Please.

A few months ago, I posted a Help Wanted ad for a graphics designer on www.Guru.com. If you've never used Guru—it's a wonderful resource! Basically, it's an online database of freelancers who are looking for work. GURU ROCKS!

Anyway, within twenty-four hours of posting my ad, I got at least 30 responses. Complete with resumes, pricing estimates and requests for further information about my project. All 30 responders seemed to sincerely want my business and not a one of them lectured, belittled or condescended to me.

Well, duh, you say, they're after your business, why on earth would they be anything but delightful in their first encounter with you?

My thoughts exactly.

Well, I've recently been lurking on Trulia.com because I've heard it's a good place to blog. I stumbled onto a discussion started by a first-time homebuyer asking questions about a particular house for sale in her neighborhood.

I was stunned at the level of lecturing, belittling and condescension expressed by the responding real estate "professionals." More than half of the responders sternly advised her to speak with a mortgage broker before "bothering" (okay, that's my word, but the message was clear) a real estate agent. Another instructed her to better educate herself on the process before looking at homes. Only two agents actually offered to show her the home, but even they seemed disinterested in becoming her favorite real estate agent.

I gotta ask…WHY are these real estate agents wasting their precious time on the Trulia forum if all they're going to do is alienate the prospects they're supposedly there to find?

Are graphics designers on guru.com more desperate than real estate agents (HA!) and therefore only grudgingly concede to being polite, enthusiastic and responsive? Whereas we in the real estate industry are so buried under a pile of qualified buyers and motivated sellers to the point where we simply don't have a minute to spare to be polite, enthusiastic and responsive?

ROFL. I crack myself up.

> "The way to gain a good reputation is to endeavor
> to be what you desire to appear."
> —Socrates

CHAPTER ELEVEN

Claiming Your Territory (Geographic Farming)

REAL estate is all about location, location, location, right? If that's the case, then it makes sense that you, a professional real estate agent, might want to claim a location (or "territory") as your very own—that is—become the go-to-guy or gal in a particular neighborhood, subdivision or market area.

Jennifer's $0.02

In some of my earlier writings, I assured real estate agents that it's possible to build a successful business "without cold-calling, door-knocking, *farming* or chasing down For Sale by Owners." So, with those words, was I implying that there's something inherently unsoulful about the subject of this chapter, geographic farming?

No, not at all, although it may have sounded that way. What I should have said was, "It's possible to build a successful business *without farming...if you don't want to.*" But there's nothing in the world wrong with geographic farming if it's a prospecting strategy that makes sense to you. Read on.

What I mean by Claiming Your Territory and becoming the go-to person is that, due to your own efforts, you have established yourself as the real estate agent to call when someone who has a home to sell in that area needs an agent. Maybe it's better to say you'd become "a" go-to person because most real estate agents will never "own" a neighborhood, simply because there are far more agents than neighborhoods to own! And of course, people who live in neighborhoods may already have existing relationships with real estate agents and wouldn't dream of calling up a stranger regardless of how heavily that stranger has marketed to them. And God bless 'em for that, right?

When you have become "a" go-to guy or gal in a neighborhood, you get business from people you probably don't personally know because your name is familiar to them…and you've made it easy for them to find your contact information. Your signs are probably on every block, hopefully with a steady progression of Available, Pending and SOLD riders atop them. Your handy-dandy who-to-call-in-case-of-emergency magnets may be on every other refrigerator. Your quarterly neighborhood newsletter is anticipated with delight, and you actually receive calls of protest if it comes out late.

This is the traditional view of Claiming a Territory—where the agent deliberately, intentionally and systematically blankets a target area with his or her marketing in hopes of becoming a household name, so to speak. In real estate, we call this "geographic farming" or just "farming." When a real estate agent selects an area to "farm," she calls it her "farm area."

"Organic" Farming

I never did much intentional geographic farming since my business model was mostly SOI. Oh, I did a little bit when my office coordinated and paid for a portion of it, but never saw much benefit.

However, during the mid-to-later years of my career I did have some fairly notable success *organically* creating a farm area—where my name was recognizable and I got phone calls from people I didn't know who considered me a go-to agent in the area. Again, not the only one, but one of the agents they invited over because they considered me a neighborhood expert.

But allow me to clarify that this was not a neighborhood I intentionally marketed myself to. I mailed zero newsletters, zero postcards and zero calendars (unless someone in my SOI lived there!). I didn't sponsor the neighborhood 4th of July barbecue or go door-to-door introducing myself. *<shudder>*

I did, however, live in the neighborhood. And loved living in the neighborhood. Which I believe was a significant factor in my success building a name for myself there.

The neighborhood I lived in, loved in and specialized in was called Northwest Denver, or North Denver or Highlands—the three names were used interchangeably. The neighborhood suited me and my personality—when I first moved there, it was considered a bit of an urban-rebellious thing to do since the neighborhood wasn't all that trendy…and I liked that. It did become trendy after a while, and still is, but it still suits me (maybe I've gotten trendier as I've grown up!).

Both because I lived there and because the neighborhood suited me so well, I understood the neighborhood—the architecture, the flow, the appeal of certain areas over others. Most of all, I understood the inhabitants and the future inhabitants. I related to people who lived in Northwest Denver and the people who wanted to live in Northwest Denver in a way I didn't relate to people who lived (or wanted to live) in the suburbs, the foothills or the more upscale areas of Denver.

So, the first step to becoming a neighborhood specialist is to choose a neighborhood to be a specialist in. Maybe the neighborhood will choose you. But if you're doing the choosing, pick an area that you like, that you "get" and, from practical perspective, one where houses are selling.

If you're running an SOI-based business, you might pick a territory where you already have friends and acquaintances or where those in your social circle might enjoy living. Not because you think all your friends will suddenly sell their homes or want to buy more but, rather, because your friends can offer you significant social opportunities to meet their friends who are likely to be of similar demographics and have similar lifestyles.

The Neighborhood Specialist

Okay, so let's say you know the area you want to specialize in. What do you think the next step might be?

Well, I'm thinking that if you're going to call yourself a neighborhood specialist, you might actually want to BE a neighborhood specialist! Actually knowing a lot about a neighborhood gives you tremendous confidence when talking about the area and that confidence will be apparent to those you are talking to...and you'll be much more likely TO talk about it when you have something to say.

So, how do you become a neighborhood specialist? Well, as we've already discussed, the best way to learn a neighborhood is to be in it. Learn as much as you can about the listing inventory by previewing frequently and deliberately (if previewing is allowed in your market). While studying data and statistics can be somewhat helpful in understanding trends, it's nowhere near as beneficial as being inside the houses and out on the streets. If previewing is frowned on in your market, take every opportunity to visit open houses and go on broker tours.

That said, do make it a habit to go thru the MLS every single day looking for new listings and recently sold properties. If a new listing looks interesting to you, take an hour and go look at it. After a while, you'll be pleased to notice you really are developing a feel for the pulse of the neighborhood.

You might consider offering a free CMA to your friends who live in the neighborhood. That will force you to analyze the market as a professional real estate agent, not to mention the practice you'll get preparing CMA's and presenting them, and not to mention the sweet little opportunity to get in front of your SOI.

Aside from the listing inventory, you'll want to understand the other features and challenges of the neighborhood. Do your shopping in the neighborhood stores and shops, walk your dog in the parks and wander through the shopping districts. Know where the nearest supermarket is. Get a feel for the school district—is it desirable or maybe not-so? And if it's "not-so," are there alternatives? If there are any challenges like airport noise or a high water table or underground toxic plumes from an old factory, those things would be good to know.

Read the neighborhood newspapers if there are any. Subscribe to the blogs or newsletters of agents who already focus on the neighborhood. Immerse yourself in learning everything you can about the neighborhood.

Becoming a Market Master takes time and it's a never-ending process, but if you commit a month or two to the process, you'll be surprised at how much you can learn even in that short period of time.

Getting the Word Out

Once you're an expert, how to you spread the word?

Not to stir up a chicken and egg debate, but the very best way to build name recognition in a neighborhood is to be doing business there. To have your For Sale signs around, preferably with a steady stream of SOLD riders on them in a reasonable amount of time. Once you have that sort of exposure, building on that recognition is much easier.

But let's assume you have no For Sale signs yet in your chosen area and no real prospects of any. What can you do to spread the word that you know your stuff (without spending a fortune)? Here are some ideas:

1. Do open houses and be super-prepared for them by previewing your heart out beforehand. If you don't have any of your own to hold open, find others to do, even if you have to do them for agents in other offices if your broker allows that.
2. If your office is in or near the neighborhood, volunteer for floor time, a lot.
3. If you've been thinking about changing offices anyway, consider finding one located in or near the neighborhood.
4. Shop in the local grocery stores and shops; get your hair cut, your nails done and your dog groomed in the neighborhood. This will give you plenty of opportunity to casually demonstrate your local expertise with the people you find there.
5. Attend local festivals or events; consider sponsoring a booth if available.
6. Eat in the local restaurants and drink in the bars; invite your friends to join you.
7. Join the neighborhood association.
8. Blog blog blog about the neighborhood and architectural styles.

9. Create a special website for the neighborhood, or a section on your website, and include a virtual tour or two.
10. If you know a lot of people in the neighborhood, that can open up all kinds of opportunities as well!

Commit yourself to both knowing the neighborhood and being in the neighborhood. And slowly, but surely, you'll build that name recognition that will bring business to you organically.

"Intentional" Farming

I just described one method of Claiming Your Territory—that of specializing in a neighborhood by becoming a master of it and then organically building name recognition as a result.

That's how I "claimed my territory" and, while it wasn't a significant part of my overall business model, my efforts were worth tens of thousands of dollars to me over the course of my career. And those efforts didn't cost me a dime, or at least, not very many dimes.

However, there is another approach to claiming a territory that may sound more appealing to you for several reasons. At the end of this chapter, we'll compare and contrast the two approaches and you can decide which better suits your personality, budget, timeframe and business model.

In November of 2010, Erica Ramus, Broker/Owner of Realty Executives in Pottsville, Pennsylvania and I held a live teleseminar discussion called, coincidently, "Claiming Your Territory." We each shared our strategies for building name recognition in our chosen neighborhoods; I described what you just read and Erica described what you're about to read.

Truthfully, the audience was far more interested in Erica's method compared to mine and I'm just fine with that. Her approach is simple, sensible and relatively cost-effective (all words that make my heart sing!). As with most simple, sensible and cost-effective prospecting strategies, we were all caught a little off-guard, slapping ourselves 'cross the head asking, "Why didn't I think of that?"

I was pretty enthralled with Erica's approach as well, and for just a minute, almost wished I were still selling real estate full-time so I could try it out myself. But alas, I'm not, so I'll let you have all the fun and tell me how it goes.

Here's how Erica develops her farm areas, one area at a time.

- **Step One:** First, she chooses an area to target. She's looking for a fairly well-defined neighborhood of 150 to 250 households. We'll talk in a minute where she came up with that number.

  The neighborhood she chooses must be active from a real estate perspective—that is—people are moving in and out. Houses are selling. Buyers are buying. Not a neighborhood where folks moved in 50 years ago and haven't budged. And not a neighborhood where houses go ON the market, but never come off (until they expire or are foreclosed upon).

- **Step Two:** Once Erica chooses her area, she creates a database of home-owners. In her market, she finds it cost-effective to pay a teenager $10/hour to input the names and addresses of the homeowners into a spread-sheet; however, there may be title companies in your market who will do it for you free or at a low cost.

  In creating her database, she eliminates the names of other real estate agents who happen to live there, but does not filter the list for active list-ings (note: if you're mailing to a general group of homeowners, there is no ethical issue including people whose homes are currently listed. It's only a problem if it appears you specifically target property owners who currently are under an active listing agreement with another agent).

- **Step Three:** Next she kicks off her campaign with a season-appropriate postcard or other mail-able piece. If it's toward the end of the year, her first mailing might be a calendar. If it's in the middle of summer, it might be a football schedule postcard. High-quality, but not overly custom or personalized; she usually uses off-the-shelf material customized only with her name, photo and contact information.

- **Step Four:** She follows up the first mailing with a second within 30 days. And a third within another 30 days. In other words, she sends out three mailings in three months. After that, she mails every other month until the 12th month, and then mails to that farm four times a year, not including her Just Listed and Just Sold announcements of neighborhood properties she lists and sells.

Her mailing pieces vary. Some are postcards, some are newsletters. Because she's mailing to a very targeted area, she's able to ensure the content is appropriate to the audience. For example, one of her farm areas is a 55+ community which might suggest a different series of mailings than would a more family-oriented one, not to mention a different type-size on the mailers!

But while the content of the mailing does matter, it's not as critical to her success as the consistency. In Erica's experience, she begins to see the fruits of her labors within about six months, although she has some sweet success stories much sooner. Either way, her farming efforts easily pay for themselves, and more, in less than a year.

In addition to her mailings, Erica also creates farm-specific websites and blogs, and promotes them in her mailings. She offers to keep the neighbors updated on the real estate activity in the neighborhood via email in exchange, of course, for their email address. She has a rather distinctive car, so she commits a little time each week to driving through the neighborhood and stopping to chat with her past and current clients if the opportunity arises.

How Much Will This Cost?

How much will you have to spend to claim your own territory?

Not as much as you might think!

The trick, according to Erica, is to keep your farms small and manageable, and do them one at a time. Don't try to take on an entire neighborhood, subdivision or zip code; unless you're independently wealthy, you'll burn through your marketing budget with your first mailing…which means you'll probably have thrown that money away.

So, how much money will you spend, using Erica's plan, if your farm is made up of 150 households?

Year One

Wages of teenager at $10/hour for data input: $30-$50
Printing #1: $50-$100 (depending on design)
Postage #1: $42—$66 (depending on size of piece)

Printing #2: $50-$100
Postage #2: $42-$66

Printing #3: $50-$100
Postage #3: $42-$66

Printing #4: $50-$100
Postage #4: $42-$66

Printing #5: $50-$100
Postage #5: $42-$66

Printing #6: $50-$100
Postage #6: $42-$66

Printing #7: $50-$100
Postage #7: $42-$66

Year One Total (7 Printings and 7 Postage): $647—$1,212

Year Two

Printing #1: $50-$100
Postage #1: $42-$66

Printing #2: $50-$100
Postage #2: $42-$66

Printing #3: $50-$100
Postage #3: $42-$66

Printing #4: $50-$100
Postage #4: $42-$66

Year Two Total (4 Printings and 4 Postage): $368—$664

So, do the math and you'll see that you can potentially claim a territory for less than $1,000, certainly less than $2,000!

Which Approach Is Right for You?

So, there you have two very different approaches to claiming a territory, although they aren't mutually exclusive. You can certainly do them both!

But let's compare the two anyway. There are distinct advantages and disadvantages to each.

Let's start with the advantages and disadvantages of "organically" claiming a territory.

To review, organically claiming a territory means that you become a recognized authority in a neighborhood because you do business there. Basically, you KNOW the area and you're IN the area. You ARE a neighborhood specialist not because you pronounced yourself to be, but rather because you, well, ARE. You know the nuances of the different blocks and boundaries. You know that houses north of Oak are worth more than houses south of Oak, and you understand why. You know the demographic and lifestyle of people who live in the neighborhood… and of those who want to live in the neighborhood. You are conversational about the benefits, challenges and political hot potatoes of the area. You understand the architecture and are familiar with the neighborhood builders. Give you an address and you'll be able to accurately visualize what sort of house sits there.

(Again, someone who intentionally farms may very well also be a specialist, as described above.)

Here are some benefits of Organic Specialization

(sounds kinda National Geographic-ish, doesn't it?):

1. You can "claim" a broader area. Because you aren't directly marketing to anyone, your area of specialization can be much larger. You aren't limited by your budget, so you could conceivably become an expert on an entire subdivision, zip code, school district or large neighborhood. My area of specialization in Denver was comprised of over 14,000 households.

2. You will have a broader knowledge of the area. By intentionally becoming a true specialist, you will be a far better real estate agent. Our product IS knowledge, market knowledge being among the most important.

Being an expert in a neighborhood or market area gives you tremendous confidence when talking about the neighborhood with both buyers and sellers.

3. Organic specialization is free, or nearly so. Let's just put it bluntly, becoming a market master is a cheap way to prospect. You may have to invest your time, but not much money.

4. Organic specialization is more fun—to my way of thinking, anyway. While creating mailing campaigns and newsletters may feel more proactive, it's not nearly as much fun as getting out there in your chosen neighborhood and really digging into it. After all, we got into real estate because we enjoy, well, real estate, right? Not to become professional mass-mailers.

5. Your results may be more enduring. Anytime you successfully market yourself organically, the results tend to be "stickier." You've earned your spot at the top, not by buying it, but by being among the best (real estate agents, not mass-mailers). It may be quite difficult for someone to knock you off that spot, especially if you keep up your good work!

6. Organic specialization allows you to mix business and pleasure. Remember some of the tips I provided to spread the word of your expertise? Walking your dog in the local park? Eating and drinking at local establishments? Attending festivals and events? There are only so many hours in the day, so if you can combine your fun times with your work times—sounds like a win/win to me!

Disadvantages of Organic Specialization

(compared to intentional farming):

1. Establishing your name takes longer. Organically claiming your territory is a long-term project, with no definable end-zone, or any semblance of a guarantee you'll ever get there.

2. It requires more investment of personal time. Consistent previewing

and studying market data takes time. You can't just devote two hours a month to creating a mailer and shooting it out. To organically become a specialist, you need to be committed to always learning more about your area of expertise.

Benefits of Intentional Farming:

1. You'll see results quicker. While it will still take time to build a name for yourself in your chosen farm (don't expect much from your first mailing or two), you'll probably start to see tangible results sooner than you will by organically farming.

2. Your results are more easily tracked. They say, "That which is measured, improves." When you're systematically mailing to your target neighborhood, you should be able to see clear correlations between your prospecting activities and your incoming leads. You may notice that one mailing generates far more phone calls than another. That your annual calendar results in more personal "thank you" contacts than your football schedule magnet. This measurable data can be invaluable to you as you continue to work this neighborhood, as well as future ones.

3. There may be a definable end-zone. Perhaps you'll set some goals for yourself with each farm to meet before you commit to the next. How many listings or maybe a pre-determined Return on Investment. You'll enjoy the satisfaction of setting goals…and reaching them!

4. Intentional farming is more proactive…or at least, it feels that way. You create a plan, you make a to-do list and then you complete that list. It just feels good!

Disadvantages of Intentional Farming:

1. The cost. No question about it, you'll spend money on your mailings. Not as much as you might have feared, but it's money that will go out the door with no guarantee of a return. And the money you commit to your farming can't be your entire marketing budget; in other words, don't put all your eggs in your farm basket.

2. You are limited by your budget. Continuing from disadvantage #1, you can only farm as much as your budget will allow. You may desire to cover a broader area, but if you don't have the funds, you can't, simple as that. And remember, your mailings need to be ongoing and consistent, so you'll need to ensure that you will have the budget to continue what you started.

3. You might not become a true specialist. Of course, this is up to you; you can certainly combine your farming efforts with mastering the market in your farm. But it's not absolutely necessary to be a specialist to intentionally farm an area, and while many agents have good intentions to become better educated about their farm, they never get around to it. And then risk looking a little silly when they get their first listing appointment as a result of their marketing.

4. It can be discouraging. Many agents have farmed unsuccessfully and deeply regret it. They resent the money they've already spent, but feel trapped by the advice to be "consistent" and the assurances that it's "just a matter of time." They wonder if they're just one more mailing from experiencing the success they're hoping for, and fear that if they give up now they'll have flushed all that money down the toilet. It can be crazy-making.

To me, this is the biggest disadvantage of all. I talk with many agents about what they wish they'd done differently their first year and almost all tell me they wish they hadn't spent so much money mailing to strangers. It may very well be that they weren't doing it "right," and would have enjoyed more success had they done something differently, but it can be an expensive gamble. Almost more frustrating than the money spent is the internal angst the agent experiences at that point where he must decide whether or not to continue. And the companies providing your mailing materials will certainly try to talk you out of it.

So…to farm or not to farm? That is the question.

"Your self-confidence is directly connected to how much
you feel you are making a difference in the world."
—Brian Tracy

CHAPTER TWELVE

Expired Listings and
For Sale by Owners

SURPRISED to see a chapter about the pursuit of Expired Listings and For
Sale by Owners here? Don't be! As an agent who Prospects and Sells with
Soul, you just might be the answer to these sellers' prayers. Seriously.

But before I write another word, allow me to make my standard disclaimer about
prospecting to Expired Listings and For Sale by Owners (FSBOs).

I never did it.

I have no experience pursuing Expireds or FSBOs (okay, I have a little experience
pursuing Expired Listings; I tried it for a few months and gave it up. Didn't like
it.).

So, feel free to discount everything I'm getting ready to tell you in this chapter,
or you can skip it all together.

However...

I have been an Expired Listing and I have been a FSBO and, what's more, I
think I have a fair amount of common sense and good judgment when it comes

to promoting one's real estate services to human beings who want to sell their homes, regardless of what category we put them into.

And that's all Expireds and FSBOs are—human beings who want to sell their homes.

Let's talk about that.

We tend to think of Expireds and FSBOs as a special kind of prospect, a special kind of seller. And in some ways, they are (and of course, if you Prospect with Soul, every prospect is special to you!). As anyone who pursues Expireds or FSBOs will tell you, these folks have raised their hands and announced to the world, "*I wanna sell my house!*" which makes them an awfully attractive target for your prospecting agenda. They aren't thinking about selling "someday;" they don't simply know someone who might want to sell; they have taken the step of actually putting their home on the market, either on their own or with an agent, which implies some level of motivation and commitment.

Neato Frito, right?

Expireds and FSBOs Are Not the Enemy!

But where I find the disconnect between agents' perception and the reality of the Expired/FSBO seller is in the assumed/presumed adversarial relationship between the agent and the Expired/FSBO seller. Agents who pursue these prospects almost universally expect and plan for resistance, to the point the agent feels the need to arm himself with scripts, dialogues and objection-busters before going in. He fully anticipates a hostile reception to his approach, and perhaps even dreads making that call or ringing that doorbell.

Whoa, talk about the self-fulfilling prophecy! Heading out into the world fully expecting to be soundly rejected by the people you're planning to pursue for business? Putting on your emotional full-body armor to protect yourself from their displeasure as you approach? D'ya think an expectation of being rejected might have something to do with being rejected?

To be fair to agents who have been rudely dismissed by Expireds and FSBOs, it may have nothing to with their approach and everything to do with the behavior of agents who have gone before them. For some reason, our industry seems to think that an aggressive, patronizing, intelligence-insulting strategy is just the ticket to persuade an Expired or FSBO seller to see the light and hire the agent using the aggressive, patronizing or intelligence-insulting strategy.

Don't get me started.

Oops, too late.

The vast majority of Expired Listing and FSBO training available to real estate agents would be comical (if it weren't so pathetic) in its utter disregard of human nature and disrespect for its target audience. I mean, puh-leeeze! To go in full-steam, armed with all sorts of graphs and charts and data created to prove the stupidity of a FSBO trying to go it alone? To call up an Expired Listing and ask him if he's "ready to choose the RIGHT agent this time?" To sweetly provide a FSBO with a pile of intimidating documents under the guise of being helpful in a transparent attempt to scare him into hiring an agent-preferably-the-agent-providing-the-pile?

Um, since when is it persuasive (not to mention polite) to insult your prospect's intelligence and competence in an attempt to earn his business?

And I have to imagine it does nothing for the agent's own self-confidence to rely on such ridiculous strategies, knowing they would never work on him. Or, among the less-soulful, to have so little respect for the potential client that she believes this nonsense will be persuasive and effective, even knowing she'd laugh at any clown who tried it on her.

An "Expert in Expired Listings"?

Speaking of, a popular Expired Listing strategy is that of proclaiming yourself to be an "expert in Expired Listings" when talking to sellers whose listing has expired. Say, what? What exactly does that mean? Perhaps you are very good at **pursuing** Expired Listings but that doesn't make you an expert in **selling** them, does it?

One day I was talking to an agent who intended to use this approach when calling expireds. I asked him what exactly he meant by claiming to be an expert.

He stuttered and stammered and came up empty. I didn't let him off the hook; I insisted he define for me what it meant to be an "**expert in Expired Listings**."

Finally he said, "*Well, it doesn't mean anything, but the seller isn't going to realize that.*"

Oh, ick.

Get Real

What's wrong with simply being authentic? Since when is it necessary to memorize a script in order to approach someone offering help? (That's a rhetorical question, of course. It's always been a part of the sales process to come armed with memorized scripts and dialogues).

But, seriously, what if you approached an Expired Listing or a FSBO with a completely different attitude? One of honest curiosity and a sincere desire (and ability) to help? Do you think this approach might:

1. give you a level of confidence no script, dialogue or pitch can ever provide and

2. be a breath of fresh air to a seller wanna-be who has been assaulted by scripted sales-pitch after scripted sales-pitch?

Because, you know what? You can help this frustrated seller wanna-be. You know how to sell houses in your market. You just might be the best thing to ever happen to him or her. Not because you have the fanciest presentation or the slickest mailing campaign, but because you know how to sell houses and you'd love to help this seller do just that.

And when you help a seller wanna-be sell his home, you get a paycheck. Win/win.

Neato Frito.

JENNIFER'S BLOG: "Mr. FSBO, You're an Idiot and I'm Not!" Yeah, That's Persuasive…

I was just talking to an agent who is going through corporate-sponsored FSBO training.

Sigh.

It's typical stuff. Under the guise of being helpful, the program advises you to scare the guy to death about everything he doesn't know about selling a house. Bring in a stack of complicated contracts and disclosures, "just so that he'll be prepared if an offer comes in." Include intimidating documents that he won't actually need just to beef up your pile. Provide a "helpful" info-sheet about the dangers of letting strangers into your home.

Again, your basic FSBO scare-tactics. And again, sigh.

Hey, someone decides to FSBO their home because they think they can do it. They think they're smart enough to do it and they don't see the point in paying some smarty-pants real estate agent a whole bunch of dollars to stick a sign in the yard and do an open house. And you know what? Maybe they are smart enough. But it doesn't matter if they are or they aren't; what matters is that they think they are. So, when you come in with your brow furrowed with faux concern and your "helpful" material in hand, all you're really doing is insulting the seller's intelligence. You're basically saying, "You're an idiot for trying to sell your house yourself! You can't possibly succeed without me because I'm so much smarter than you are."

Oh, I know that's not what you're saying, but that's what he's hearing. And we wonder why FSBOs can be hostile to us smarty-pants real estate agent types!

How about being straight with the guy? If you think you can help him sell his house, then prove it. Be helpful without strings attached. Authentically care about his situation instead of mastering that furrowed brow. Be willing to walk him through contracts and answer his questions. Contrary to popular belief, demonstrating your expertise by sharing your knowledge won't eliminate the seller's need for you. I hope not, anyway; if it's so easy to sell and close a house that we can explain it in an hour or two, that seller truly DOESN'T need us!

Being cheerfully and genuinely helpful and caring will go a whole lot further with a suspicious FSBO than all the scare tactics in the world!

For Sale by Owners

Voices from the Real World of Real Estate

Contributed by Lisa Petersen, www.DLPHomes.com

My FSBO technique is really quite simple. Each morning I go on to Craigslist and sort the By Owner listings for homes added the previous day. I send each owner a simple email complimenting the home and asking if they'd be willing to pay my company a commission if I bring a buyer who purchases the property.

This often results in a positive response and I make an appointment to preview the home. Before arriving, I preview the competition so I'm prepared in the event they want to talk shop, and I bring a simple market snapshot analysis of what's happening in the neighborhood. I don't go in with any intention of talking about listing their home; I leave the data with them and encourage them to contact me if they have any questions.

This has been a nice, relaxed way to begin a conversation. After the initial meeting, I ask permission to send them updates on the market and I check in every week or two to see how it's going.

I have never asked to list a FSBO home; they've asked me.

Why Does Someone Try to Sell a Home on His Own?

To save the commission? Yeah, probably. In most cases, that's exactly why someone goes the FSBO route, although there may be a variety of sub-reasons they feel FSBO is the best route for them. But it generally comes down to their opinion that we real estate agents aren't worth our fees.

And you know what? Many of us aren't. Would you pay someone thousands of dollars to put a sign in your yard, do some simple data-entry, drop off some typo-infested home brochures and hold an open house or two? I wouldn't. (Well, that's a lie, I have, and I begrudged every dollar. Perhaps your FSBO prospect has had the pleasure of begrudging his dollars, too).

So, assuming your FSBO prospect has had a negative experience with one of "us" or has heard tales of such negative experiences, it's understandable he might think it an abysmal waste of money to pay us to do what he can probably do himself. Gone are the days where we held the keys to the MLS; most markets allow FSBOs to hire "entry-only" or minimum service companies to get them access to the MLS. So with that obstacle removed, it actually is feasible that a FSBO can get just as much exposure for his listing as a substandard real estate agent will.

BUT THIS DOESN'T MEAN HE'S CATEGORICALLY OPPOSED TO PAYING A FULL REAL ESTATE FEE!

He's just not willing to pay "full-price" for minimal, amateur or substandard service.

Many agents, particularly newer ones, consider approaching FSBOs with a proposal to list their home for a lower-than-their-typical fee. They come up with a fair buyer agent co-op and add a little on top for themselves. Their rationale makes sense—since the seller will likely have to pay a buyer agent anyway, surely he'd be willing to add a little more to be represented by a full-service real estate agent, right? And the agent (particularly a newer one) gets much-needed exposure, experience and a little something in his pocket at the end of the day.

I have mixed emotions about this strategy, but this is not the time or place to explore them. For our purposes today, let's talk about whether it's even necessary to "buy" a FSBO's business with a low fee.

It's not.

Here's the thing. A FSBO just wants to sell his house, no different from a retail seller. He's FSBO-ing for any number of reasons, but at the end of the day, he wants to go to a closing and move on with his life. As we discussed, he probably doesn't feel that a real estate agent brings enough to the table to justify his or her thousands of dollars in fees.

But if the real estate agent COULD demonstrate his value; if he COULD assure the seller that he:

1) knows how to sell houses,
2) can likely recapture at least his portion of the real estate fee in a higher sales price, and

3) will make the process much easier and hassle-free than the seller can do on his own…

    …the seller may just be willing to consider paying the agent's full fee!

Of course, therein lies the challenge! How do you demonstrate to a FSBO (or any seller prospect for that matter) that you are worth your fee?

Hmmmmmm?

Ready for Some Tough Love?

If you can't answer that question for a FSBO (or any other seller prospect), it's time for some serious soul-searching. If you don't believe with all your heart and soul that you earn your fee (note, I didn't say that you NEED your fee), then, frankly, I think you should hang up your real estate license until you do. Without the conviction that you are a good real estate agent, that you are someone worth the money you hope to be paid, you will fail, and deservedly so.

xoxoxo

Pursuing Expired Listings

Okay, enough melodrama. Let's talk specifically about Expireds now.

The biggest challenge to pursuing Expired Listings seems to be that initial contact. Not just working up the nerve to make that first contact, but also whether to mail, call or drop by. How to find the owner's phone number. How to get around the Do Not Call List. What to write in a letter that will inspire him to pick up the phone and call.

And of course, what to say when you do call or drop by?

I don't have any pat answers for you. In some situations, you'll call. In others you'll write. From time to time you may show up in person. If you intend to pursue Expired Listings, you'll have to figure that out, and there are plenty of other programs, systems and tools to help you. My friend Borino's Expired Plus program (www.expiredplus.com) gets into the initial contact in great detail (as well as all the other pieces and parts of the process).

What I will share with you here is what would have worked on me during the periods of my life when I was an Expired Listing myself. And perhaps within those words you'll find your answer, that is, what would work on YOU if you found yourself in the position of the person you're considering prospecting to?

A handful of times, I've had properties of my own listed that, for various reasons, expired.

And I tell ya, the expired campaigns that resulted from my listings expiring were pretty darn cheesy. Obviously the agents were taking a shotgun approach to getting business from us poor saps who desperately needed their "professional services." Textbook Numbers Game—throw enough doo doo against the wall and eventually something will stick. And most of it was, indeed, doo doo.

Here are some examples of the cheesy marketing I've gotten from agents who wanted a shot at my Expired Listing:

- Daily postcards addressed to "Property Owner."
- Postcards with a hand-written "Call me! I Have a Buyer for Your Property!" (Uh, the house was on the market for 9 months before it expired last week!)
- Envelopes with my name misspelled (at least that's a step above "Property Owner").
- Letters with promised "enclosures" missing (e.g., "Enclosed is a list of homes that have recently sold in your neighborhood!")
- A laughably cheesy series of letters with an insulting, condescending tone.

When agents called me on the phone about my Expired Listing, they were obviously calling from a list and were not in the least bit prepared for a real live human being to answer the phone. They were usually nervous, probably due to the fact that they were not at all ready to intelligently discuss the specifics of my listing. I guess they were just shooting for the appointment, and didn't bother to "waste any time" in preparation.

Real Estate Agents Ask...
"How do I...?" Ask ye-self first!

Every day, every hour, a real estate agent asks "how to" do something. How to... approach a FSBO? How to...better market a listing? How to...target first time buyers? How to...persuade a seller to reduce his price? Etc., etc., etc.

Good questions, all. Deserving of answers.

However, I believe that in most cases, the answers are within ourselves. Not that I mind being asked (I love sharing my—*ahem*—brilliance), but a big part of the SWS philosophy is to learn to Trust Your Gut. To know that you can (and should) listen to your own instincts and intuitions!

So, with that said...

If you were a FSBO, how would you like to be approached by a real estate agent? What would catch your attention? What would turn you on (or, more importantly, off)? What would inspire you to want to work with one particular agent over another?

If you were a First Time Home Buyer, how would you go looking for an agent? Where would you be likely to stumble upon one? What sort of marketing would catch your eye?

If you're wondering how to sell your difficult listing....ask yourself...If I were a buyer, or a buyer's agent, what would inspire ME to give this listing a chance? Conversely, why might I be avoiding this particular listing? Of all the listings available to show my buyer, what could the listing agent do to convince me I should show THIS one (because remember, as a buyer agent, I only get paid when my buyer buys, so I only wanna show the BEST)?

If you were an upside-down seller, what might your agent do to convince you of the need for a price reduction? How would you like him or her to approach you? What sort of information might be helpful and what attitude would be effective?

When faced with a dilemma that involves another warm body, put yourself in the other fella's shoes. And act accordingly...

Here's the thing.

The owner of an Expired Listing may really want to hear from you...if you have something to offer aside from a cheesy canned marketing pitch and a desperate desire to get a listing agreement signed. These people are not the enemy—they're, yes, real live human beings who have a need they'd love you to fill. But no mass-mailing or mass-calling campaign is going to convince anyone you're the right (wo)man for the job.

What to do instead?

Quality over Quantity

Instead of simply shoveling out postcards, brochures and missing enclosures to as many targets as possible, take the time to personalize your approach to a few. Drive by the home. Take a close look at the expired MLS listing. Note any marketing challenges you see and think about how you would address them. See if you can identify why the home didn't sell—it may be price, but it very well may not be. Try to figure out if the property is a short sale; that will affect your approach. Ask yourself, "Can I sell this home?"

That's what your target audience wants to know. Can you sell their home?

If I had received just one personal letter (and I don't just mean a hand-written envelope) from an agent who had taken the time to actually look at my situation and address it specifically, that agent would have had a great shot at my business. If one of the agents who called me actually knew where "Doe Run Estates" was located and why it's special (and yet challenging), I'd have been impressed. If any of them had indicated they had a clue why my property didn't sell, or even a sincere desire to find out, they might have caught my attention.

But, sigh, no. All attempts to entice me to take the next step were in vain. Hopefully they had more luck with their 99 other targets-du-jour...

What's the Punch Line Here?

Well, if you were expecting a step-by-step process for prospecting to FSBOs and Expireds, you're probably a little disappointed. Sorry 'bout that. But my goal has never been to simply tell someone how to run their business, but rather to inspire them to create a business that's all theirs… that they're proud of… that feels right and that they can maintain without changing who they are.

However, I understand that you may feel you need a little more guidance in creating a plan for pursuing FSBOs and Expireds. The good news is that there are plenty of programs out there for you to consider. The bad news is that many of them are truly awful. As I mentioned earlier, Borino's Expired Plus (www. expiredplus.com) is one of the good ones and while it's specifically focused on Expired Listings, I believe the concepts can be easily tweaked to work with FSBOs as well.

And I'll leave you with that thought. If you ever purchase a program, system or tool to help you succeed (even one of mine), do not hesitate to make it your own. Embrace that which resonates with you; reject anything that does not. Change anything in the system or program to better suit you. Ignore anyone who advises you to blindly follow their program.

Just nod, smile politely, and do it your way.

"Isn't it surprising how many things, if not said immediately, seem not worth saying ten minutes from now?"
Arnot L. Sheppard, Jr.

CHAPTER THIRTEEN

Soulful Social Media

I almost didn't include a chapter about online social media in this book. Crazy, I know, especially since everyone tells you that you must participate in social networking in order to survive as a real estate agent in today's world.

So, why did I considering excluding this chapter?

First, by the time the words I write today hit the bookshelves, whatever I say about social media may very well be obsolete. Today, Facebook and Twitter are the most recognizable and mainstream platforms of social media exchange, but in a year that may not be the case. And I'd sure hate my readers to roll their eyes and say to themselves, "This gal is SO last year—no one uses Facebook anymore!" Not sayin' that'll be the case, but when was the last time you heard anyone mention MySpace?

Another reason I debated including a social media chapter was because, while I have a familiarity with some social media, I'm no expert. I count myself among the crowd who "doesn't get it," especially when it comes to Twitter. I've tried, I really have, but as of this writing, I still don't intentionally Twitter. I think my blog is set up to automatically Tweet when I post something, but otherwise, eh, my followers on Twitter don't hear much from me.

Yet another reason I thought I'd just pass this topic on by is that plenty of other people in our industry have discussed it in depth and continue to do so. And since I'm not an expert or even a big fan, it made sense to me to simply declare my ignorance and ambivalence and refer you to others who have more information and passion than I do.

Well, in the end, you're reading a chapter in *Prospect with Soul* about social media. Guess I changed my mind.

Sort of.

I'm going to talk about social media from a somewhat general perspective. A philosophical one. You won't find many specific tips or detailed instructions in this chapter about how to organize your friends on Facebook or create lists of your followers on Twitter or post your resume on LinkedIn.

Okay?

Reconnect with Old Friends

I believe one of the best uses of social media is to reconnect with your old friends…as an old friend. Not as a real estate agent looking for business but someone your past and present friends know or knew, who happens to sell real estate for a living.

In my Savvy Prospector program (an eight-week self-study course about creating a sphere of influence business model), I advise agents to write what I call a "reconnection letter" to their spheres of influence, which kicks off their new and improved sphere of influence business model. Some agents have balked at this, feeling a little silly about suddenly sending a letter to someone they haven't spoken with for months or even years, worrying that their audience will be suspicious of their out-of-the-blue attempt to get back in touch.

Well, not to debate whether or not that's a reasonable concern, but either way, social media is a wonderful solution to this dilemma. You can join in on conversations or simply say hello to old friends and acquaintances and if it's done sincerely, without a hint of a sales pitch, no one will think twice about it.

"If You Don't [blank], You'll Fail..."

BAH!

Is anyone tired of hearing this line? Lately it's all about Twittering, Facebooking, LinkedIn-ing and whatever other latest technology I'm not familiar with. A speaker at a recent Colorado REALTOR® Rally proclaimed an agent's Number One marketing tool was...YouTube!

HUH?

Of course, it's not as if we haven't been hearing this same message forever. In the old days (and still some today), the Masters proclaimed that if you don't cold-call, door-knock, farm or advertise, you'll be dead in the water. Next you had to bombard your Sphere of Influence with cheesy mailers every month. Then you had to have a fully functional website. Then you had to SEO and PPC. Oh, and you must have a PDA (the old-timey Daytimers won't cut it). Gotta have a blog, mobile-web and GPS...

OR YOU'LL FAIL!

Nonsense. I guarantee you that if I never Twitter or go near my Facebook page again, it will not affect my success selling real estate. And I'm still enamored with my trusty Franklin Planner (the paper kind), with no plans to upgrade to digital.

Just do what has always worked for you! Upgrade to new technology when YOU'RE in the mood, not when some guru scares you half to death with the consequences if you don't!

"If I don't Twitter, I'll fail..." Sheesh.

Besides, using social media solely for socializing is perfectly fine; I'm not saying that you must use it for business, although, if done properly, it can be a great source of business for you. But not because you're blatantly marketing yourself or even subtly marketing yourself (which is rarely as subtle as you might think), but rather because, as we discussed in the Be Pleasant chapter, you're making someone's day just a little brighter by stepping into it.

And therein lies the secret to successful social media-for-business. Log in with the intent of making other people smile.

How do you make other people smile? Two ways.

First, you comment on their posts, pictures and notes. Show an interest in them and their lives. If they post something clever, express your appreciation at their cleverness. If they post something sad, express your sympathy or support. If they ask for help or advice, offer some if you can. If they post something self-congratulatory, congratulate them, too. In short, join in and participate in their conversations, without any hint of a sales pitch or mention of your real estate business.

The second way to make people smile is to post your own clever or otherwise commentable non-sales-pitchy updates. The old joke about social media is that "no one wants to hear what you had for breakfast" is absolutely true, but I'm sure your life is much more interesting than that! Be transparent, be authentic and be interesting. If you can't think of anything transparent, authentic or interesting to post, then just comment on others' updates until you do. Your "status" line doesn't have to be up-to-the-minute up to date!

Be Authentic (without crossing the line)

Don't be afraid to share some of yourself on social media platforms. You don't have to be formal, professional or 100% proper when online; in fact, don't. It's fine to share the good news AND the bad with your online friends. When my mother died, I posted it on Facebook and received dozens and dozens of sweet comments from my online friends.

Of course, there's a fine line between being authentic and sharing the too-personal details of your life. Never forget that the people who keep up with you online can potentially lead you to your next $10,000 paycheck, so if your updates are primarily angry or frustrated or angst-ridden, you're not going to create the RCHB persona that's so important to generating business from the people you know.

You'll have to figure out that line for yourself; I can't give you any hard and fast rules. But here are some tips:

Don't post or comment about:

1. Your frustration with your wife or husband (unless it's clearly light-hearted)
2. Your despair over your real estate business
3. Your anger at a client or associate
4. Your hangover
5. Your depression over your recent divorce
6. Your dating life (don't be changing your "relationship status" every other week!)
7. Your sex life (or anyone else's)
8. Your too-busy life
9. Fund-raising for your favorite cause

To contrast, here are some personal things that may be perfectly fine to post or comment about:

1. The death or illness of someone close to you
2. Thankfulness for good news from the doctor (for you or someone close to you)
3. Yay, me! If you win an award, are interviewed in the media or have a particularly good month or quarter
4. Tales of your dog(s) or cat(s)
5. Asking for advice or referrals (to others, not for yourself!)

One more word about social media platforms—never forget that your friends have the ability to "hide" or remove you as their friend if you irritate them with self-promotional or otherwise spammy posts. Don't give them any reason to consider doing that!

Be an Online RCHB

Another great use of networking online is to meet new people to impress with your RCHB'ness. Not necessarily your real estate wonderfulness, although it might come up, but in other areas of your life as well. If you're highly interested and/or a bit of an expert in, say, growing orchids or showing horses or counseling runaway teens, find online venues and groups to participate in that allow you to meet like-minded folks with similar interests.

Politely join in on conversations or start some of your own, all the while being aware that the other members of the group don't care one bit about your real estate career—at least, not yet. Once you've established yourself as a bona fide member of their "club" and someone they feel they know, like and trust, there may be opportunities to mention your real estate career from time to time. Or, as other members get to know you, they might even check out your profile and discover what you do for a living without your bringing it up!

Since real estate is a location-based career (location, location, location!), it makes sense to look for like-minded groups or conversations of folks who live in your market area by looking for conversations about local issues or events that interest you enough to participate in online conversations about them. Janie Coffey (www.thecoralgablesstory.com), my go-to-gal for all things social media, advises online networkers to initiate face-to-face meetings with their online "friends" as soon as it feels comfortable to do so. She assures us that the other person will be honored that you're interested in meeting and is probably just as excited about meeting you, assuming you have a bona fide online connection.

I'm sure it goes without saying that you should never approach an online friend (or any friend, for that matter) with the sole goal of prospecting to them. How would you like it if the chiropractor or accountant or massage therapist or mortgage broker in your online network or group or conversation called you up one day with the clear intent to sales pitch you on his or her product or service? Or, perhaps worse, waited until you were face to face before whipping out his fancy charts and graphs of how you could make a gazillion dollars by joining his network of gizmo-gadget salespeople?

Your goal in social media networking, as with all networking, is to broaden your base of people who know you, and may eventually know that you sell real estate. Not to find as many people in the world to assault with your sales pitch.

I know you know that. Forgive me for assuming otherwise!

Asking for Help Online

Another less-intuitive approach to meeting new people on social media is to go looking for help from the online community. Perhaps you want to become an expert on orchids or horse-showing or teen-counseling, but don't know much about your interest other than, well, you're interested in it!

People like to help other people, especially if they get to demonstrate their expertise to an appreciative audience. BE that appreciative audience. I know how warm and fuzzy I feel toward people who sincerely ask me for advice and give me every indication that they're going to put my advice to use. Because they clearly respect MY knowledge, experience and expertise, I think they're pretty smart, since I have a healthy appreciation for my own knowledge, experience and expertise!

Don't Spam Your Sphere

Right here is where I should write a treatise about the dangers of spamming your online sphere of influence with sales-pitches, announcements of new listings, or pleas for business and referrals.

I really don't have to do that, do I? I didn't think so. Don't do it. Don't do anything in social media that might be construed as spamming. If you aren't sure, just don't.

Can you mention your real estate career? Sure. But do it less than you'd like and with great care. Again, when in doubt, don't.

Voices from the Real World of Real Estate

Contributed by Janie Coffey, GRI

Here are some Dos and Don'ts of Selling with Soul on Facebook.

DO…

1. *use the comment or "like" button to let others know you are reading their status updates and you agree, share their pain or just enjoyed them. People love to know they are being read.*

2. *follow your friends' updates to see what their interests and hobbies are; it is much easier to build a solid foundation for a relationship with someone when you share a common denominator.*

3. *use Facebook to alert you when a friend's birthday is coming up (but don't use Facebook to wish them a happy birthday. Everyone else does and your wish will get lost in the shuffle. Give them a call instead).*

4. *post interesting information that you think your friends might find interesting and useful (but don't overdo it; Facebook is more about the interaction than just posting tons of links).*

5. *be yourself, flaws and all; it allows people to feel comfortable with you and build trust in you as a "real" person, not a marketing version of yourself.*

6. *use the "chat" feature to say hello to people you haven't spoken to in a while.*

7. *create "groups" so that you can filter who you send certain updates to. For example, if you are having an open house, or know of a great sale coming up, you might want to update your local friends on this. You can create as many groups as you want. Do this early in your Facebook life; you will be glad you did.*

DON'T…

1. *use Facebook as a spam media to post your listings relentlessly. If you have a nice one, you can, of course throw it in, but the quickest way to be "un-followed" is to post nothing but real estate over and over again. Seriously. Facebook is the most personal and relaxed social media and anything perceived as hard-selling is taboo.*

2. *allow the games like Mafia Wars, Farmville, etc., to post your updates. You can still enjoy these, but honestly, no one else cares what level you reach, who you knocked off or what tree you harvested.*

3. *stalk people, or anything that could be perceived as stalking—use the "if it quacks like a duck" test.*

4. *tag people in photos without their permission. Not everyone likes to have pictures of themselves posted that they haven't seen before or like.*

5. *be upset if someone doesn't accept your friend request. Some people keep their Facebook very private and some rarely use it so there are lots of reasons (not related to you) that could explain their reasoning. Let it go.*

6. *get so addicted that you stop making personal contact (calls, direct emails, etc.). Facebook does not replace more personal contact with your Sphere, only enhances it.*

7. *take it personally if someone interacts less than you'd expect or hope; as mentioned above, everyone has their own Facebook protocol. Facebook can be as much or as little as you want it to be. If used with care and mindfulness, you can learn more about your friends (both personal and professional) while introducing them to a deeper level of yourself, both of which can build better relationships. This can build trust and deeper connections that can help build your SOI, one friend at a time.*

"In business you get what you want by giving other people what they want."
—Alice MacDougall

Chapter Fourteen

From Online Lead to Real-World Client

"Internet Leads Are a Total Waste of Time!"

HAVE you ever said or thought this? Ahhhhh…keep reading.

In Chapter Seven we talked briefly about responding to inquiries that come in to you via email as a result of your advertising of a specific listing (that is, an Internet "sign" call). In this chapter, we're going to dig much deeper into working with incoming leads that are generated by your website, specifically your IDX (or other property search feature).

In other words, leads who come into your life because they did a generic search for "<Your City> real estate" or something similar and found themselves on your website.

How you get yourself in this position (that is, having a website that online buyers find themselves on!) is beyond the scope of this book, and by the time you're reading this, anything I write today would be obsolete anyway. But for our purposes here, let's assume you have a website that enjoys a fair amount of traffic, and that you have a system in place to capture (either actively or passively) the contact information of your visitors.

So, how can you turn that contact information into a client, and later, to put it bluntly, a paycheck?

At least 90% of what follows in this chapter is provided courtesy of my friend, Matt Jones, founder of FavoriteAgent.com, and is compiled from Matt's books, blogs, articles and interviews. While I'm no expert on converting Internet leads, I know common sense when I see it and Matt's insights and philosophies on the topic of working Internet leads definitely sound sensible to me!

So, thank you, Matt, and to you, dear reader, I hope you enjoy this little infusion of testosterone!

Matt Jones Sez...

Way back in 2004, the National Association of REALTORS® determined that 77% of our real estate customers were using the Internet for at least some part of their home searches. And that number has obviously grown since then; current estimates place that figure at over 90%.

So let's take a look at these Internet homebuyers. Here are some things you may want to know about them, compared to "non-Internet" homebuyers:

- They're better educated.
- They have more money.
- They're buying more expensive houses.
- Their search time is shorter.
- They like to help in the process.

They sound like the perfect customers, don't they? However, they're also more demanding than their predecessors and they want information today. Tomorrow's not good enough! They go to the Internet to get that information, and if you're not there, someone else is.

If you want to claim a piece of this business for yourself, it's imperative that you have a strong web presence, that you learn how to capture business from the web, and, most importantly, that you know how to respond to today's Internet customer.

Internet Real Estate 101

Let's talk about the nature of Internet leads. How are they different from other leads, such as referrals or duty-desk leads? Should you handle them much as you would sign calls? Or should you treat them more like open-house leads? How should you approach them? Are they all the same?

The Real Estate Buying Cycle

An agent who has historically been successful in a traditional real estate model is frequently unsuccessful when he tries to transition to Internet leads. Then, because the veteran agent isn't successful with Internet leads, it's tempting for him to assume the leads must be of poor quality.

But that's not true. The reason many veteran agents have problems working web leads is not because the leads are of poor quality but, rather, because they approach Internet customers as if they are typical customers coming from other traditional marketing (i.e., sign calls, referrals, calls from farming, duty-desk calls). But web leads are much different—not different in the sense that they're not buying or selling homes, but different in the sense that they're coming in at a *much earlier point* in the real estate buying cycle.

And it's a fundamental misunderstanding of the 21st century real estate buying cycle that causes many agents to fail with Internet leads.

So let's talk about the real estate buying cycle and how we can change the way we approach and follow-up with real estate customers on the Internet.

The real estate buying cycle consists of three phases:

Phase One: Information-Gathering

Phase Two: The Search

Phase Three: Escrow (or Contract to Closing).

This buying cycle has been relatively unchanged for many years but, until recently, very few agents knew that Phase One even existed.

- *Phase One: Information-Gathering*

    Research indicates that home-shoppers begin the process (Phase One) of buying a house about 4-6 weeks before the beginning of Phase Two, or 6 to 8 weeks before the beginning of Phase Three.

    During the early part of Phase One, the buyer is thinking about budget, features and amenities, neighborhoods, and school districts. He's fantasizing about the American Dream of home ownership which he considers a mark and measure of success, and thus wants to be careful and thorough. In this initial phase, the customer is solidifying, in his own mind, what he wants to buy. He chooses his search criteria and his budget (although often incorrectly, as any experienced agent can tell you!).

    This is a very important part of the buying cycle, and it's going to happen whether we're aware of it or not. **Most importantly, Phase One of the buying cycle is the only part of the process that customers want to do on their own**. Our clients don't want to have their dreams shaped by agents, parents, friends, or anybody else. They want the dream to be theirs. This phase is going to last 4-6 weeks. Anyone attempting to speed up the process does so at his own peril!

- ### *Phase Two: The Search*

  After the information-gathering phase has run its course, the buyer proceeds to the next phase and a mental shifting of gears. He's determined what he wants and is now on a legitimate quest to find it. This phase typically lasts about two weeks (yes, just two weeks!).

  It is at this point that real estate shoppers understand that they need a real estate agent to help them in the process of finding their dream homes. But what they don't want (and I can never reiterate this enough) is for us to try to shape their dreams. That part of the process is very personal for most customers.

  During the search phase (Phase Two) of the buying cycle, the customer wants to look at real live houses. He'll typically do lots of drive-bys on his own and will begin skimming through home magazines. Remember: he now knows what he wants and is out to find it. And, somewhere in the middle of this search phase, he wants to begin working with an agent.

  This is the crucial part of understanding the buying cycle: the agent who's on the customer's mind when he reaches Phase Two is the agent who's most likely to close the transaction and collect the commission!

So how do you become that agent? By being there! You need to be there at the precise moment the prospective buyer decides it's time to find an agent. That moment he calls a duty desk and asks to see a house or picks up a home magazine and calls the listing agent or is out driving around looking at neighborhoods and decides to call the number on a sign.

Interestingly, this is the point many agents have traditionally picked up their new customers. Well, the customer hasn't changed with the advent of the Internet. What has changed is when the customer first comes into our lives.

Phase Three: Escrow

Beginning with the acceptance of the contract and moving forward to closing, there's the third and final phase of the buying cycle, also known as the escrow or contract-to-closing phase. As this is a chapter about converting Internet leads to clients, we won't cover this phase here.

This is one of the most important things to take away from this discussion. If you learn nothing else, I hope it's this: Internet leads come in during Phase One!

Has the light clicked on? Has the aha! popped into your head yet? According to the National Association of REALTORS®, 76% of all buyers will work with the first agent they talk to. If we're first, the odds of our doing the deal are 3:1 in our favor. Period.

What a huge advantage! A smart agent will simply identify the customer first and then devise strategies to make sure he doesn't mess up the process. The rest will take care of itself.

Here is a simple yet powerful illustration that may change the way you look at Internet leads.

I want you to think back to the last time you shopped in your favorite department store. Now, if you're like me, you don't have a lot of time to waste; when you go shopping, you go because you want to buy something.

But remember how, as you walked into the clothing department, a sharp sales clerk came up to you and asked, *"Can I help you?"* Now, I want you to be completely honest—what was your answer? You know what it was; it was the same as mine: *"No, thanks. I'm just looking."* And I'm willing to bet that, within five minutes, you were looking around to find that same clerk to help you locate something in your size.

But when you answered, *"No, thanks. I'm just looking,"* did you really mean that you weren't interested? Or were you implying that you wanted to gather information for a few minutes, but later you might need assistance? The process is no different for a real estate customer except that the buying cycle is much longer, given the price point and complexity of the purchase. But the point is that the Internet customer is still gathering information when most agents who pursue Internet leads call to ask, "*Can I help you?*"

There are generally only two reasons an agent fails with an Internet lead: either he'll take the "*No, thanks. I'm just looking*" literally, as though the customer wants nothing to do with him, or (more often) he won't take the hint and insists on pushing for an appointment to start showing houses. This overbearing, hard-sell approach simply alienates the potential customer and removes any chance of the agent gaining the business. But make no mistake: that customer will go on to buy, but with another agent! What a tragedy.

Is there a solution to this fundamental problem? Of course.

The first step is to embrace the reality that the Internet is a legitimate source of business and is here to stay. At the current rate of growth, virtually all real estate customers will use the Internet for help in their property searches in the near future. As real estate professionals, we can either accept that fact and capitalize on it, or we can begin to "build our parachute" and look for an exit.

The next step is to understand the real estate buying cycle and know that customers don't want us around much during Phase One. Around, no—in touch, yes. But not in a pushy way. We need to master the skill of being visible but not pushy. Our job is to be helpful. What could be simpler? Learn to serve your customers, without asking anything in return. You are simply there to make a friend. Research (and common sense) shows that a home buyer will work with an agent that he likes, so be that agent. Your job is simply to make him like you during this crucial first phase.

Finally, the third step is to have a follow-up system in place that will allow you to maintain contact with these "future" customers over a longer period. The rule of thumb is to keep it short and keep it personal. Mix it up. Use phone calls and personal emails; twenty to thirty words in a short but personal email will do much more good than any mindless drip campaign. Let's be honest, we all know a drip campaign email when we see it, and so will our prospects. We owe it to them to become personally involved.

When you're tempted to dial-up the pressure with your Internet prospects, remember this simple truth: three-fourths of our customers will use the first agent they talk to, assuming they can remember who that was. So stay in touch, but stay out of the way, and the odds are 3:1 that you will earn a commission.

Serve, Don't Sell

When calling online leads, you're most effective using a customer-service approach. Offer service and friendship, not a sales pitch. In other words, don't try to personify the "super-agent" Real Estate Professional. When you act like a typical salesman with your prospects, you'll get a typical salesman's response from your prospects.

So, let's get specific. Here's an example of what you might say when calling a new online lead.

"Ms. Smith? Hi. This is Matt with ABC Realty. I've noticed that you've visited our website while looking at houses online, and I'm just doing a customer service follow-up call to make sure that you were able to find everything you were looking for."

[Pause for a response, which is normally a little cool.]

"I wanted to let you know that I'm not calling to try to sell you anything."

[A noticeable sigh of relief here.]

"Actually, I'm calling to make sure that you aren't having trouble with the MLS search on the site or if you have any questions about it. Oh, by the way, you're going to love Fayetteville. We have a really great city—lots to do, lots of shopping, great schools. So what part of the country are you coming from?"

The purpose is to begin finding common ground and building a new friendship. As your lead warms up, you'll notice a change in receptivity. At no time do you try to set up an appointment, show houses, get a mortgage lined up, or in any way make it a traditional sales call. Simply begin building a relationship on this call. That's its sole purpose. Allow the customer to set the pace, choose the topics, etc. When the natural conversation begins to run out of gas, you might conclude with something like:

"One more thing, if you like, I can set up a service for you where we take the features

you're looking for and put them into our computer. Then, whenever a house comes on the market that meets your criteria, we send you the listing by email. The service is free, and I can set it up for you in no time."

The prospect almost always wants this service. The reason for offering listings by email is that it gives you a good excuse to call back and strengthen the relationship.

"Okay, great! I'll check back with you in a few days to make sure you're getting the listings by email and to see if we need to change any of the search criteria."

After this first phone call, staying in touch is crucial. Remember, 76% of all buyers work with the first real estate agent they talk to. So if you don't make the customer mad at you (by being a pushy salesman), you have a great chance of getting the business and a commission.

What Phase Is the Buyer in?

First things first. Before you do anything else, you need to determine where the buyer is in his buying cycle. If he's in Phase One (and he will be in Phase One about 90% of the time), you must use a very hands-off and nonthreatening approach. If the buyer gets even the slightest inkling that you are trying to shape his dream, push him, manipulate him or sell him, he'll be gone so fast it will make your head spin! Trust me, I know from experience.

How will he disappear? Normally he'll leave you in a very non-confrontational way. He'll tell you he's changed his mind and isn't going to buy. He'll not answer your phone calls, because he recognizes your phone number. He'll not return your messages. He'll report your email as "spam" so your future correspondence goes to his junk folder and he never even sees you again.

Some persistent agents will try different strategies, like calling from a different phone number or using a different email account. What does this communicate to the customer? That the agent is desperate or worse, that he's pushy (which is why he started ducking the guy in the first place)!

A Phase One buyer must be approached with kid gloves. He's skittish. He's easily spooked. And you only get to fail once, because the reason he's on the Internet is because he wants to be "out of touch" until he's ready to move to Phase Two.

As someone who sold for a living for over twenty years before coming into the real estate business, this went against everything I had ever known. As salespeople, we are all taught the ABC's... Always Be Closing.

But I promise you one thing — if you use traditional sales approaches on Phase One leads, you will be frustrated, and you will probably decide that Internet leads are bad leads.

I approach a Phase One buyer with the goal, not of getting an appointment, not to sell him a house, but rather to make him like me. My definition of a successful call to a Phase One buyer is that he takes my next call!

Phase Two buyers, on the other hand, want to work with an agent. When you encounter one, you can be direct and pull out all the stops. If you don't, you'll lose your potential buyer to a more aggressive and skilled agent.

So how do you know which phase your potential buyer is in?

It's best to assume the buyer is in Phase One and use the customer service approach. If he wants to go faster, he'll let you know. Better safe than sorry, I always say. There is little risk in erroneously assuming a Phase Two buyer is in Phase One. The worst that can happen is that the buyer might surprise you and want to meet sooner than you'd expected.

But there's a huge risk in assuming a Phase One buyer is in Phase Two. You risk alienating your lead and never having the opportunity to work with him at all.

Staying in Touch—What to Do and When to Do It

Now that we've identified where your customer is in his buying cycle, let's discuss some basic theories of what to do and when to do it, although I'm deliberately not giving you word-for-word scripts. I want you to learn the theory and not some rote presentation. If it sounds canned, it is by its very nature, not personal. Friendship is personal and I want you to befriend your potential customers.

Having spent years training sales people, I know that a) most people will never learn a canned approach well enough for it to sound natural, and so it will come across to the customer as disingenuous and phony; and b) as simple as this approach is, it is much better to teach the theory and allow you to make up your own "scripts" as you go. That will allow you to focus on being a friend and not on selling.

Let's start by answering the "when" to do it, and then we can cover the "what" to do.

You should touch Phase One customers twice a week and Phase Two customers every day. How you touch them is not as important as the frequency. If you attempt to touch a Phase One customer more than twice a week, you will come across as needy and desperate, and worse, pushy.

Remember, our objective in prospecting is to make the potential customer like us. If the approach we use has the exact opposite effect, we shouldn't use it, **even if it's easier**. We'd be better off doing nothing than using an approach that moves the relational ball the wrong way down the field. Resist the urge— it doesn't work anyway.

Communicating Via Email

There are two simple rules I use in my email marketing: keep it short and keep it personal.

I have a friend who writes thousand-word epistles to her prospects, believing that by being verbose she will win them over. There is an abundance of research on the subject, and the consensus is that less is definitely more. Try to keep your prospecting email correspondence around 50 words or so, until and unless it is in response to a specific request.

Personal is always better than impersonal. I try to recount some personal reference or anecdote to let my reader know that it is not a canned email. Three or four good personal, well-thought-out sentences will do more for advancing your relationship with a potential customer than thousands of words of cold, impersonal, drip campaign letters will ever do. If you can't be bothered to take the time to write a personal note, you really need to rethink your profession. This is a very relational business.

Communicating on the Phone

Email is a great way of maintaining a relationship, but it is not very good at initiating one. The reason should be self-evident. Email is less personal than talking. For that reason I believe that our personal conversations with our customers are more important than our email campaigns. Voice carries with it emotions and subtle signals that are nearly always absent in writing. Our emails are often cooler and come across much differently from the message we were attempting to communicate.

My own rule of thumb* is to always make my initial contact with a new Internet lead by telephone. Until I speak to someone, I won't write an email that might be considered spam. Once we have spoken, I have a "history" that I can refer back to in a very innocent way to communicate that the email is not a canned drip mail.

I'll leave you with a final note on the subject of phone calls. Always leave the seed for your follow-up call. On my first phone call I will generally say I will do my best to call in a week or two to check on the emails (that we're setting up with her search criteria) and to see if we need to refine anything. I let the buyer know it is pretty normal to have to tweak the search a few times until we get it just right. That lets him or her know I'll be following up and it gives an expectation that I can then exceed.

Then I set an activity in my contact manager and call back in one week. Exactly.

The first thing I say is, "*I know you didn't think I'd call, but I promised you I would so I did.*" Then we discuss the search criteria and we are like old friends. I'll talk as long as it is comfortable but won't overstay my welcome. As the late jazz singer Sammy Davis Jr. said: "Always leave them wanting more."

We as real estate agents often try to make it too difficult. Let's face it — the buyer wants to buy (it's the American dream), the seller wants to sell, the lender wants to lend, the closing attorney wants to close, the inspector wants to inspect — it doesn't get much easier. If we simply focus on making friends, exceeding expec-

---

* Matt's registration form requires the user to include a phone number. That's his preference and it works for him. You can certainly choose to make the phone number field an optional field if you like; however, in Matt's experience, voice-to-voice contact is far more effective, especially during that very first contact.

tations, and serving our clients, we will be rewarded greatly. It couldn't get any better!

What a great business we are in!

And Now a Few Words from Jennifer...

So, there you have it. A plan to convert Internet leads into clients. Like everything in the Prospect with Soul philosophy, working Internet leads is largely a matter of common sense, respectful behavior and good manners. Approach these leads as you would like to be approached if you were beginning the process of searching for your next home.

If you'd like to chat with Matt Jones directly, or learn more about his lead capture program and software, he'd be delighted to hear from you! Just track him down at www.LCMsuccess.com, or check out his blog at www.blogmattblog.com.

"Success is not to be pursued;
it is to be attracted by the person you become."
—Jim Rohn

CHAPTER FIFTEEN

Cold-Calling, Door-Knocking & Related Nonsense

ARE you surprised to see a chapter about cold-calling and door-knocking?

Well, it'll be a short one and, for the most part, entirely unhelpful if these are the sorts of prospecting techniques you're interested in.

I probably don't need to define for you what cold-calling and door-knocking entail. But what the heck.

When you cold-call someone, you're calling up a total stranger who has not indicated any interest in hearing from you, and asking for business. Regardless of whatever cute & clever pitches you come up with to justify that your call has value to the ~~poor sap~~ person on the other end of the line, that's the point of a cold-call. Asking for business.

When you go out a'door-knocking, you're basically doing the same thing 'cept you do it in person. Which, in my opinion, is even worse. You're disrupting someone in their home, their sanctuary, and asking them for business. And very likely disrupting them from doing something they'd much rather be doing, or need to be doing; certainly something more important (to them) than talking to you. Even if that "something" is taking a nap or watching SportsCenter. Unless they're really, really lonely, of course; then your visit might be a welcome distraction in their day. But then YOU might regret knocking on that particular door!

What cold-calling and door-knocking are not (and this might ease your mind a bit) is calling on an Expired Listing (within the legal limits of your local regulations and/or the Do Not Call (DNC) list) or a FSBO (ditto). While your call or knock might still not be the highlight of the recipient's day, I believe you have a bona fide reason to make contact, and if you also have a bona fide interest in actually helping the person who answers the phone or the door, your contact might even be appreciated.

So, when I preach against the cold-call and the door-knock, I'm not including the pursuit of Expired Listings and FSBOs in that "do not" list. Just wanted to make that clear.

Neither do I have any real issue with dropping off brochures or flyers at houses in a neighborhood. As long as you don't ring the doorbell and impose your pitch on an unwilling party, go ahead and drop away.

(I'm not saying this is a good use of your time, but since I never did it myself, I can't really comment on its effectiveness, and aside from my dogs going nutso when someone enters the perimeter of my yard, I don't have a problem finding brochures or flyers on my front door.)

But when you pick up the phone at 8:00 a.m. every morning and begin dialing random phone numbers and asking the poor guy who answers if he knows anyone buying or selling real estate, and when he says he doesn't, you promptly hang up and dial another number…and another…and another…that's cold-calling.

And when you cruise thru a neighborhood armed with your mega-watt smile and faux "homeowner survey" and personal brochures, insisting you're providing value to the folks who come to the door when you ring…that's cold door-knocking.

But Jennifer, it WORKS! I know it annoys people, but I get a lot of business from cold-calling and door-knocking!

Bully for you. Lots of things "work" but that doesn't make them right. I hear that cocaine will perk you up if you're feeling a little sleepy, but I don't advise it as a solution for the mid-afternoon blahs.

Would you rather annoy 30,000 or impress 300?

If you hang out with me much, you know how I feel about the traditional numbers game of prospecting, specifically cold-calling.

Blech.

A business model based on being rejected far more often than you're welcomed and calling it a game?

Blech.

I don't think anyone who cold-calls imagines that his or her calls are welcomed by the majority of the voices on the other end of those telephone lines. When you commit to a cold-calling business-building strategy, you have to acknowledge that you will annoy a lot of people. But that's okay, they say, because the end justifies the means. It's okay to annoy a lot of people as long as you end up with a little business for yourself when the day is done.

So, I'm thinking.

What if, instead of striving to ~~annoy~~ cold-call 100 people a day, you strive to impress one person a day?

At the end of the year, the cold-caller will have annoyed more than 30,000 people...but you will have impressed more than 300.

Who do you think is a better source of future business for you? Thousands of annoyed people? Or hundreds of impressed people?

You Have My Blessing to Cold-Prospect...

...If, and only if, you truly appreciate being cold-called yourself (and you aren't on the DNC list). And if, only if, you truly enjoy being interrupted in the privacy of your home by a door-to-door prospector, you have my blessing to cold-call and door-knock to others. It doesn't mean I want you calling me or visiting my house, but it IS part of the Prospect with Soul philosophy that it's okay to prospect unto others as you would like to be prospected unto.

Prospecting in the Age of the Do Not Call List

A few years ago, I was interviewed by REALTOR® Magazine about Prospecting in the Age of the Do Not Call List. Specifically, what recommendations I, Jennifer Allan, queen of cold-calling (*snort*) might have for agents stymied in their prospecting efforts by that pesky DNC.

We had a great conversation, although I doubted my brilliance would make it into the final article since I really had no experience with the DNC except for being first in line to sign up.

(I was pleasantly surprised to learn that it did. In fact, they gave me my own article, along with a spot on the cover!)

But one of the last questions the interviewer asked made me think...and I came up with an answer off the cuff that I was rather proud of. Thought I'd share it with you.

Question: *"Jennifer, I understand that you never cold-called, but I'm sure that someone in your RE/MAX office has. If that agent were to ask you for advice on what to do instead, what would you have advised him?"*

JA's Off-the-Cuff Answer: *"Ummmmmm."*

No, seriously, I did come up with something...

"What I would probably tell him would be to get out from behind the desk and the telephone and take his naturally charming self out there into the world and make contacts face to face. No, not by knocking on doors or attending power networking events, but rather by striving to make a positive impression on as many people as

possible as he goes about his day. By implementing a Quality over Quantity approach to attracting business. Instead of trying to make contact with 100 people a day, who will almost certainly promptly forget about him, try to really connect with two or three, who will be much more likely to remember him tomorrow...and six months from now."

I'm guessing that someone who has experienced success in cold calling has an appealing personality and a confident aura of success, which would be very attractive out in the real world, too! And, frankly, being out in the real world making real friends and real connections sounds a whole lot more fun and rewarding than dialing for dollars three hours a day!

I must confess that while I think my advice is brilliant, I've never been approached by a master cold-caller for my opinion and I don't expect to be in the near future. So, while I don't see the cold-calling world to suddenly shift their tactics to the PWS-Way, I do hope I can inspire those who'd rather not cold-call to try the PWS-Way and see if they like it!

Which leads me to my next point.

Are You Being Pressured to Cold-Prospect?

What if your office pushes cold-prospecting (calling and/or knocking) and is insisting you participate?

Well, you'll never, ever hear me say that you should go ahead and try it (you might like it!) if your gut is screaming in protest. Which I truly hope it is, by the way.

There are a few different ways to gracefully handle the situation.

Option I: You can smile sweetly, give the impression of being on board, and completely ignore the pressure. It IS your business, after all.

Option II: You can politely, but firmly explain to your broker/trainer/manager that you're a fan of the Golden Rule and since you don't enjoy being cold-called yourself, you simply won't do it to others.

Either of these options is perfectly fine, by the way, as long as you combine it with a plan to find yourself some business using methods more acceptable to you. Because you do need to be doing something, obviously! If you have a viable Plan B, your broker will probably leave you alone.

But if the pressure to participate gets so intense that it's affecting your confidence or your emotional well-being, you might have to change offices. And rest assured, there are plenty of other real estate offices that promote less-objectionable prospecting methods, or at least, leave you alone to do things your way.

A Perfectly Reasonable "Excuse" Not to Cold-Call!

I'm doing a little one-on-one consulting with a relatively new agent. We have similar personalities when it comes to our feelings about prospecting and business-building, so our conversations about prospecting always lead to some interesting aha! moments for both of us.

Yesterday, my agent friend told me about a conversation he had with a like-minded career coach—one who specializes in matching personality types with business-building strategies. According to this coach, my friend is capable of cold-calling and door-knocking for business, and he might even be rather good at it, as long as he feels he has something of value to offer.

HOWEVER, the coach cautioned him that even though he might be moderately successful in his cold-prospecting efforts, his personality type is simply not one that tolerates rejection well over the long term. That if he spends too much of his time and energy on prospecting activities that involve a steady dose of rejection, he'll eventually become depressed and discouraged. And probably won't realize why he's so lethargic and unenthusiastic about his career...and his life.

That makes perfect sense to me! I've been preaching for a long time now that there's no reason to spend your days doing something that you aren't comfortable with when there are perfectly acceptable alternatives. And if there AREN'T perfectly acceptable alternatives, maybe you're in the wrong business!

The good news, of course, is that there are plenty of real estate prospecting techniques that don't involve much rejection. Oh, sure, rejection is a part of life, but that doesn't mean you have to put yourself in positions of pursuing it in the name of generating business if you don't want to. There's no need to "suck it up" or "just do it" if the sucking-up or just-doing makes you miserable.

Life's way too short for that. Figure out what you enjoy doing that brings in business. Do that. It really is that simple.

INTERLUDE: DO YOU BELIEVE IN YOUR PRODUCT?

A friend of mine is registered as an affiliate of a multi-level marketing company, that is, she sells the product and also recruits other people to sell the product under her. It's not her passion; she's a full-time real estate agent by day and reluctantly agreed to sell the product upon heavy influence by her brother-in-law. But, lo and behold, she had some success and, as she describes it to me, is just a few new recruits away from maximizing her "down-line" and making big bucks just by waking up in the morning.

But she just isn't doing whatever it is she should be doing to get those last few down-line recruits. Every time I see her, she bemoans the fact that she just can't seem to get motivated to make a sales call or hold an informational seminar or even to follow up with the leads she has.

I faced a similar situation recently. I was offered an incredible opportunity to get in on the ground floor of a new company that promised to take the nation by storm. My primary responsibility would be to "develop my region," which, as you might infer, is a fancy term for "recruiting."

I unofficially accepted the position. My ego was pleased—I had the fancy-schmantzy title of "Regional Director," and, according to the promotional material, the earnings potential was darn near unlimited.

Yummy.

My first assignment as Regional Director was to put my business plan together. Okay, fine. I can do that—I love to plan.

But I couldn't. And I didn't. And I couldn't and didn't some more. I fell asleep every night worrying about my business plan and woke up every morning hoping I'd get the energy to attack it that day. Four weeks went by and no business plan cometh. Why? Well, I finally admitted to myself that, even though the underlying concept of the company was interesting and the personal financial potential was great, I didn't fully understand or embrace the business model.

I finally gave my notice for a job I'd not even begun. And haven't regretted it for a minute.

My point? As a Soulful Prospector, you need to believe in your product to be able to sell it. Do you? Do you believe in your product?

Um, Jennifer, what exactly IS my product?

Great question!

Contrary to what you might be thinking, the product you're selling isn't property. You don't sell houses, condos, land, apartment buildings or mobile homes. Sure, you're involved in the sale of these products, but you don't actually sell them.

The only product you sell is yourself—your knowledge, your expertise, your work ethic and your commitment to serve your client.

So, I'll ask again. Do you believe in your product? Do you believe you're the best agent you can be? Do you sincerely feel that your clients are lucky to have you as their representative?

If you don't believe you are a great product; if you think your clients could do better elsewhere, no prospecting technique will work for you long-term. Maybe not even short-term.

Of course, we all have insecurities. All of us. Some of those insecurities are grounded in reality, some are left over from childhood or teenage melodramas that seem kinda silly now. But in general, you must believe yourself to be a good choice of real estate agent for your potential clients if you want to stand a chance of prospecting to them convincingly. If you believe they're only doing you a favor by hiring you, your prospecting efforts will likely crash and burn.

So, in order to Prospect with Soul, you need to get yourself to the point where you know in your heart (and soul) that you are, indeed, an exceptionally fine product!

"Safest way to get what you want is to deserve what you want."
—Billionaire investor Charlie Munger

C H A P T E R S I X T E E N

The Very Best Prospecting Method on the Planet

'VE been preaching and teaching and writing about and even pitching products since 2006 on how to run a sphere of influence-centered business, based on the people you know and the people you meet, instead of based on how many strangers you can prospect to on a daily basis. So, many of my readers make the logical assumption that I spent my entire career socializing, lunching, mass-emailing, going to Walmart with a smile on my face, popping into the bank instead of the drive-thru—all those things I've been telling my followers to do.

Well, guess what? After my first year (which is when I implemented my successful take-a-friend-to-lunch campaign), I didn't do much of that at all. In fact, if you go back through my tax returns from 1998-2006, you'll find very few entertainment expenses.

Sure, I did some mailings, and when email came along, I was pretty good about doing my monthly mass-emailings; I tried to attend client housewarming parties and I went to a handful of obligatory social events with my husband but overall, my on-purpose SOI activities were next to nothing.

Why? Because I was slammed busy with buyers and sellers. All my working hours were filled with doing things my clients needed me to do and I frequently pulled all-nighters to catch up on my paperwork.

But you know how many of those hours were spent prospecting? NONE.

Or, maybe I should say, ALL.

I've always claimed that my business was nearly 100% SOI—that is—obtained from people I knew or met, as opposed to from traditional methods. But you know what? Most of that business was, indeed, from my SOI, but it was from the subset of my SOI who had used my services or knew someone who had. In other words, the majority of my business, after my second year, came in as a result of **client** repeat and referral business.

When you're doing a good business, people often ask you where your business comes from. This question always perplexed me because I didn't have a snappy answer. What I usually said was, "My phone rings, I answer it, and I have a new client." And that was pretty much the truth. And I'm sure that sort of business model doesn't happen simply because you're good at taking people to lunch or sending out newsletters.

In 2001, as one of the top-producing agents of the year, I was interviewed by my RE/MAX franchise's newsletter as to the Secret of My Success. To paraphrase, here's what I said:

"I'm at the point in my business where I don't really need to prospect anymore. I have a good referral base, so I have plenty of time to focus on taking care of my clients..."

Conversely, another top agent was interviewed and here's what she said:

"I would say the key to my success would be prospecting. I make 45 calls per day, every day, no exceptions."

I remember seeing her "Secrets" and thinking, "Wow—she's been around a while, why is she still prospecting?" It comes back to one of the basic mantras of Selling and Prospecting with Soul: *"The clients I am honored to have today are far more important to me than the clients I hope to have tomorrow!"*

So, what did I mean earlier when I said that I **never** prospected, but I **always** prospected?

Well, I mean that everything I did, every day, to better serve my current clients, was effectively prospecting to them. It was ensuring their future business and their referrals. No closing gift, no anniversary card, no referral-begging or annual calendar is going to inspire that kind of loyalty.

Okay, enough about me and how wonderful I am. Let's talk about you. What can YOU do to impress the heck out of your clients so that they'll do your prospecting for you?

Do You Believe?

First, you gotta believe it—believe that the best way to ensure future business is to take great care of the business you already have. And that might be a bit of a project on its own, right? We've been so brainwashed into believing that Job One is to prospect that it might be hard for you to get into the mode of putting your current clients first on your priority list.

Impressing Your Clients

There are a million things you can do for your current clients to impress them. Even if you only have a few buyers and sellers, you can keep yourself busy all day long taking care of them. And you should! Instead of always thinking of ways to prospect for new business, try to shift that energy to thinking of ways to take better care of the business you have.

When you get up every morning and sit down at your desk with your cup of coffee, go over your client list first thing. Your buyers under contract, your active buyers, your active sellers and your sellers under contract. Don't forget your back-burner buyers. Is there anything any of these clients need from you, or would like from you, or would be pleasantly surprised to get from you?

Um, Jennifer, like what?

Like…

1. Would any of your sellers appreciate an open house this weekend?
2. Have you previewed the competition around your listings lately?
3. Do any of your sellers need a phone call, even just to say there's nothing going on?
4. Do you have any showing feedback to pursue and/or share?

5. Have you offered your time this weekend to your active buyers?
6. Have you checked in with your buyer's lender to see if he's been in touch with your buyer lately?
7. Have you previewed new listings lately for your back-burner buyers?
8. Have you checked with your sellers to see if they need more home brochures?
9. If you have any vacant listings, have you checked on them lately?
10. Have you called the buyer's agent for your listing under contract lately for any news you can report to your seller?
11. Have you provided updated market reports for your sellers?
12. Have you checked your MLS listings lately to make sure they're still accurate and that the photos are still in season?
13. Have you asked your buyers-under-contract if they'd like to look at the house to measure for window coverings or appliances?
14. Have you refreshed and/or shared your advertising with your sellers?
15. If you have a listing that isn't selling, have you spent some quality time trying to figure out why?
16. Have you reminded your buyer-under-contract about getting home-owners insurance bids or switching over the utilities?
17. If you're the buyer agent on a short sale deal, have you followed up lately with the listing agent?

I could go on all day. And I hope you could, too. These are all things that you are being well-paid to take care of, and believe me, your clients know you're being paid well—in fact, they probably think you're better paid than you actually are, so you want to live up to their expectations instead of trying to convince them that you shouldn't have to.

This is an important point. If something is important to your client, and they've shared that with you, don't try to talk them out of it—just do it, in most cases. I don't care if you think open houses are a waste of time, do at least one and see how it goes. If it's a disaster and your seller wants you to do another, think before you refuse. If your buyer wants to go back to a house for the third time with his second cousin to get another opinion, just do it. An awful lot of what we do to earn our money is done behind the scenes, so anything you can do that your client will see you doing is almost always a good use of your time.

You Only Get One Chance…

This seems like a good time to talk about first impressions. When you start working with a new client, whether it's a buyer or seller, you, to quote the old cliché, only have one chance to make a first impression. But let's take it a little deeper than that. The first impression is so powerful that even if later you drop the ball or show up less than prepared, you'll probably be forgiven.

I'm not talking about coming on strong during the sales pitch period and then vanishing afterwards which is what a lot of agents do. I mean you do everything in your power to blow the sox off your new client upfront. Don't take shortcuts; don't make excuses, don't hope that some carelessness will be overlooked.

For example—when you go out with a buyer for the first time, be sure you'd previewed everything you're going to show him and have memorized how to get from house to house. Make sure your car is clean. Be on time, dress nice. Don't give yourself anything to apologize or make excuses for. Cover your bases.

With your new seller, once you have his signature on the listing agreement, that's the time to really make a great first impression. Get the marketing in place immediately, send him a copy of your virtual tour, send him a copy of the MLS listing, get those home brochures delivered as soon as possible. Follow up aggressively for feedback on the first showings. Be in touch every day for the first week or two.

Of course, this doesn't give you permission to do a fantastic job for a week and then ignore your client, obviously. And I don't think you would. But again, a positive first impression will do wonders for the opinion the seller or buyer has of you, even if you slip a little down the road, which we all do.

What if I Don't Have Anyone to Take Great Care of?

So, what if you're new or just really slow right now?

I have to admit, I feel for new agents these days. When I started my career in 1996, we were in a boom market and buyers were everywhere. They didn't all buy because good listings were few and far between, but a new agent could definitely find buyers to work with, and impress, even if those buyers didn't lead directly to a paycheck.

Today I know that's not the case. So, building a business based on wowing your customers may not happen as quickly as it did for those of us who began our careers during boom times. By the end of my second full year, I'd sold more than 50 houses, so I had a sweet little database of past clients already. You may not have that luxury. But the approach of wowing your clients is still an awesome way to prospect, even if it doesn't pay off as quickly as you'd like.

So, the best I can tell you is to take the philosophy to heart and when you do have yourself a buyer or a seller, take care of them as your first priority. First, it'll keep you busy, and activity leads to more activity and, second, it will impress that buyer or seller and I promise it'll feel great to get a referral from them, even if it's the only referral you get this month.

What Isn't Impressive

Let's talk for a minute about things that don't necessarily impress a client. Two things come to mind.

First, a fancy closing gift.

While there's nothing in the world wrong with giving your buyer or seller a nice gift at the closing, don't do it in anticipation of it generating future business and referrals for you. Many agents agonize over finding the "right" gift that will remind their client of them "every time they see it" so they'll remember to send referrals the agent's way.

But here's the flaw in that philosophy. If you did a great job for your client, they'll remember you fondly. If you did a lousy job for your client, they'll remember you…not-so-fondly. Doesn't matter what gift you did or didn't give them; it won't change their impression of your competence and refer-worthiness. As we discussed earlier, you DO need to stay in touch with your past clients so that they know you're still in real estate, and they know how to find you, but a closing gift should not be done with the intent to impress. It should be done with the intent to thank or congratulate.

The second thing that doesn't impress a client is fancy, systematized post-closing follow-ups. Many agents take their paychecks and run after closing, breathing a sigh of relief that the deal is done, especially these days. Hey, I do it, too.

Then they put their past client on some sort of automated system to send them greeting cards at their anniversaries, and add them to their general marketing database. Fair enough.

But, right after closing and in that next month is a perfect time to continue to take great care of that client. If it's a buyer, call him a few days after move-in to make sure everything went okay. It probably didn't, so you may be hesitating to make that call. Yet this is a perfect opportunity to continue your service to him, even if that paycheck is already safely in your hot little hand. Whatever problem your buyer had or is having, you can probably help. Maybe he needs your handyman, or maybe something wasn't as it should be and you need to open your checkbook and fix it—these are golden opportunities to stay in your buyer's good graces instead of trashing all those warm fuzzies the buyer had toward you because something went wrong in the end.

You Have My Permission to Impress

I just shared some specific ways you can impress your clients in hopes of generating future business and referrals from them. However, the point of this chapter isn't so much to teach you HOW to blow your clients' minds with your attention, but rather to give you permission to do so.

Permission? Huh?

Yes, permission. Because you've probably been subjected to some degree of traditional sales training, you've probably heard all about how to focus your efforts on activities that bring in more business so as to ensure a full pipeline. You've heard how what you do today affects the business you'll have 90 days from now. The point being that if you're aggressively prospecting today, you'll see results from that prospecting in your pipeline three months from now.

Therefore, according to this approach, any spare time you find on your hands, you should be using it to prospect. Fillin' up that pipeline.

Fair enough. However, please consider a slightly different approach.

Your prospecting activities—whatever those may be—should be positioned **behind** taking excellent care of your current prospects and clients. Don't hesitate to go above and beyond when the opportunity presents itself. Answer your phone after hours and on weekends when you can. Return phone calls promptly even when it's inconvenient. Every once in a while, drive all the way across town to deliver something you could have gotten away with faxing or emailing. Call your client after the closing to find out if she needs anything from you or has questions. Offer to make a phone call for her that she seems uncomfortable making. Heck, volunteer to check in on her cat when she goes on vacation!

Think about it. Here is a warm body who has taken a chance on you. She's, perhaps, forsaken all others because she's made the decision that you're the best (wo)man for the job, and she hopes to God she's right.

Now, who better to focus your efforts on—someone who may not even know you and has absolutely no loyalty or interest in helping you build your business? Someone who won't believe a word of your self-promotional material because she's heard it before? Or, someone who has already honored you with the opportunity to impress the hell out of her by living up to the promises you made?

It seems like a no-brainer to me. Don't squander the chance to create a raving fan by placing prospecting to strangers ahead of serving your current clients! Exceptional service is rare and in our industry the bar is set very low, unfortunately. But the silver lining might be that going above and beyond will definitely be noticed!

JENNIFER'S BLOG:

"We Got What We Paid for and Were Happy to Pay It"

As you may know, my mom died a few months ago. It's a rite of passage we all go through, I know.

When someone dies, there are immediate details to take care of. And these details must be attended to right away, regardless of whether it's convenient or even bearable to deal with them. Even as your heart is breaking, you must attend to these gazillion details, and usually (hopefully) without much experience to draw from.

Well, even in the midst of my family's sadness at Mom's death, I must confess to a little sticker-shock at the prices associated with one's final journey. We're a practical bunch and agreed on a pretty basic package, but the final tally was still somewhere between $10,000 and $15,000.

I thought it was quite a racket. $500 for a tent and seating at the graveyard? $1,500 for a concrete vault? $900 for this and $1,200 for that? Not to be disrespectful, but sheesh. I was starting to feel a little taken advantage of.

Well, when all was said and done, I was wrong. Or, at least, pleasantly surprised (if you can use the word "pleasantly" in relation to your mother's funeral) at what we got for our money.

Kent, our wonderful funeral director, took care of us. Very good care of us. Exceptionally good care of us. In our time of need and sorrow, he showed up. And handled everything he possibly could. Professionally, competently. No unneeded drama or stress on a family who didn't need any additional drama or stress. The service and visitation went flawlessly, even with last-minute changes and requests. When the cemetery claimed to have no record of our plot reservation, he took care of it. After the family left the cemetery, he stayed behind to ensure that the final step in the process was completed without incident. When we returned to the funeral home after the burial, our things were collected and waiting for us.

But, Jennifer, what's so impressive about that? After all, you paid him to do a job and he did it. Big deal, right?

It was a very big deal.

Because...we toss around the phrase "You get what you pay for" as if it's an undisputed fact. But it's not. In fact, I very rarely pay top dollar for something and feel I got my money's worth. Most of the time, I feel ripped off. I usually come away with the conviction that the person I paid a lot of money to has an inflated sense of his or her own worth, and that I was taken for a ride.

But every once in a while...someone blows me away. They DO their job and they do it well, and with pride. They deliver.

What's my point?

My point is that we real estate agents also charge a lot of money for what we do. Thousands of dollars. And our fees are almost universally perceived by our clients as excessive, perhaps even a racket, at least at first.

But we have the power to take that perception and turn it around. To deliver on our promises! To take care of the details! To show up and do our jobs, professionally, competently. Without subjecting our clients to unneeded stress or drama, which they certainly don't need.

We charge a lot of money for what we do. But if we do it well, exceptionally well, maybe our clients will say of us: "I got what I paid for and I was happy to pay it."

"Do what you do so well that they will want to see it again and bring their friends."
—Walt Disney

C H A P T E R   S E V E N T E E N

Putting It All Together

AS I'm pulling together this chapter, I must confess that I struggled throughout the writing of this book with one simple concept...What's the punch line?

By that I mean that I wasn't sure where I was going with all the advice that was flowing through my fingertips. While I believe with all my heart that what I have to say is valuable and worth listening to, I wasn't confident that I could pull it together at the end to make a lasting impression on you and your real estate career. I definitely didn't want to be one of those writers who tells a good story but doesn't provide enough meat for her readers to actually implement the ideas presented.

On the other hand, I meant what I said earlier when I promised you I wouldn't be providing a "system" for you to implement—Step One, Step Two, Step Three and voila! You have a successful real estate business! I just don't believe it's that simple, for anyone, natural salesperson or not.

So, here I am, in the final chapters of the book, wondering how I'm going to tie everything up in a pretty bow so that you're satisfied you got your money's worth.

I'll let you know when I figure it out...

Nah, just kidding.

I do have a plan for you, but you need to know that it's not a simple linear process of following Step One, Step Two, Step Three and so on.

Rather, it's a process of evaluating all the pieces and parts I've presented to you throughout this book, of figuring out which pieces and parts apply to your business model and market and, further, which feel right for your personality and talents. It's a process of trial and error—of trying various techniques and tracking the results. Of making mistakes. Of making discoveries. Of learning new things. Of abandoning old paradigms.

Growing a successful real estate business is a project that will never be done! But let's get started anyway…

First Things First—Where Has Your Business Come from in the Past?

Take a minute to look at your client and prospect lists from the last few years and write down where each client or prospect came from, that is, how did they find you (or vice versa)?

See any patterns or common denominators? If most of your business seems to come from one or two specific sources, you're probably already well aware of the power of those sources. And it would only make sense to continue working those sources, whatever they are, perhaps even working them harder, rather than taking them for granted.

But, for many of us, business comes in from a variety of sources; perhaps a combination of word-of-mouth, advertising, an online presence, open houses or FSBOs.

So, make a list of how every client or prospect crossed your path, and note how many times that particular source of business shows up on your list.

Next, you might want to analyze the costs of each business-generating source. Unless you're made of money, I assume you'd prefer to maximize your bang-for-buck results. Blogs are (usually) free, while advertising and mass-mailing are typically not free. So, if you find you're getting the same return on investment for both, for example, you might consider doubling your blogging efforts while paring down your advertising and mailing promotional budget.

For example, if you find that advertising in a local paper brings in business, but you're just breaking even on the cost, that is, the business it brings in pays for the advertising, but not much more—it's worth considering whether or not that is a good use of your money. Or whether you can tweak your advertising to work harder for you since obviously it is working, just not hard enough.

Whatever's working for you already, do more of that. If something isn't working for you, let's backburner that activity while you explore new avenues of generating business. Especially if it's costing you money!

Review Your Current Marketing Materials

I have a product called "The SWS Listing Analyzer for Expired Listings," which helps agents evaluate Expired Listings to figure out why they didn't sell. The Analyzer process begins with the simple things, such as, did the sellers require unusual notice for showings? Was the MLS description accurate? Did the sellers insist on being home for showings?

Sometimes it can be something as easy to fix as a jammed lockbox to get a previously non-selling home sold. Sometimes it's something more complicated and/or expensive to correct. But I encourage agents to always look for a simple solution first.

It's the same way with your marketing materials. There might be some simple little tweak or correction that will make all the difference in the world. Maybe your website "Contact Me" page isn't working or is going to the wrong email address. Maybe the phone number on your email signature is incorrect. Maybe your outgoing voicemail message is uninviting or off-putting. Maybe your SPAM filter is on overdrive and you're missing emails from potential clients!

Or, you might find you need to make some more significant changes. Likely, you'll find a combination of both.

Make a list of every single marketing item or venue you are currently using to market yourself. This includes your:

- Business card
- Blog
- Online profiles
- Website
- Newsletter
- Newspaper advertising
- Email signature
- Personal brochure
- Outgoing voicemail message
- Photo

It's highly likely your current marketing contains errors or outdated information. It's likely some of it is dull. If you have an online presence, it's likely your various profiles, blogs and sites have missing photos or broken links. (It happens to all of us!)

Commit an hour a day to going through your marketing materials and begin making needed improvements and corrections. If you need to jazz up your business card, find a hungry graphics designer to create something gorgeous for you cheaply. Read through all your existing online profiles to ensure that they're still an accurate representation of who you are and what you do. Go through your website with an eagle eye looking for broken links, missing pictures and outdated information.

Try www.guru.com for graphics design and web assistance. It's a website where you post your project and gets bids from interested providers. I've had great luck with it!

If you do any print advertising, take a good hard look at it. Is it well-designed? Accurate? Up-to-date? (But, most importantly, is it working?)

Read through your personal brochure if you have one, asking the same questions, including, yes, is this marketing piece producing results?

Call your own phone number and listen to your outgoing voicemail message. Is it friendly? Confident? Welcoming? Or too long, too brusque or just plain off-putting? You can win (or lose) a lot of customers simply on the strength of your voicemail voice.

Look at your email signature if you use one. Is it still accurate? I see a lot of signatures that include non-functioning links.

As you find areas that need improvement, commit to making the improvements as your time and budget allow. And again, make your decisions based on how effective each marketing piece has been for you. If you've had little or no success with your website, that's probably not an area to focus on unless you have deep pockets for a total overhaul and new marketing program. Conversely, if you've had some success with your website, but not as much as you like, it might be worth investing some money into the design and searchability.

Decide Which New Prospecting Activities You'll Try

Okay, so you've figured out what you're doing that's working…and you'll do more of that perhaps. You've figured out what's not working…and you'll do less of that perhaps. So, what else can you add to your mix?

Well, to review, here are all the prospecting strategies described in *Prospect with Soul:*

- Sphere of Influence (including RCHB-ing, Being Pleasant and Staying in Touch)
- Mastering Your Market
- Floor Calls, Sign Calls & Internet Inquiries
- Open Houses
- Blogging
- Neighborhood Specialization/Geographic Farming
- Expired Listings
- For Sale By Owners
- Social Media
- Internet Leads
- Providing Exceptional Service

How's Your Phone Voice?

Like most of you, I talk to other real estate agents on the phone pretty regularly. Some in the course of my real estate business, some in the course of my writing, training and speaking career. And I tell ya—there are a lot of unfriendly voices out there.

Within an hour the other day I spoke with two different agents, about two totally different topics. The first was calling me to ask about some Open House signs I had listed on Craigslist. He was distant and dismissive and didn't seem much interested in having a conversation with me. The second was calling for information on a listing and she was delightful. The kind of voice you'd like to ask to meet you for Happy Hour, and be pretty sure you'd have a wonderful time.

Last week, I participated in a couple of Real Estate Week online seminars in which all participants had the opportunity to chat one-on-one with other participants on the call. The difference among the various voices I was matched up with was striking. Some of the voices were hesitant and unsure; some were bold and somewhat abrasive and a few were warm and inviting. I naturally have fond memories of the warm and inviting voices; not so fond memories of the others.

Hey, I'm the last one to tell someone to change who they are, but it's a fact that many of your clients and prospects are going to judge you by your phone voice. Of all the real estate agents I've spoken with on the phone this week, only two or three of them would have inspired me to pursue a professional relationship with the person, had I been in the market for a real estate agent.

If you can stand it, record some of your phone conversations. Then listen...and see how you feel about both the warmth and confidence of this person (that would be you!). Try to be objective—I know it's hard—on one hand you hate the sound of your voice, but on the other, it's tough to admit that perhaps you sound a bit unsure or, conversely, brash.

You might also pay closer attention to the people you speak with on the phone, whether they're in the biz or not. What is your impression of this person? That they're confident? Competent? Caring? Knowledgeable? Or bored, scared or clueless?

It sounds trite, but if you stand up (or sit up) straight when you talk on the phone, put your shoulders back and smile, your phone voice will improve exponentially.

By the way, when the afore-mentioned "distant and dismissive" agent came by to purchase my open house signs later in the day, he was quite pleasant in person. But that phone voice...ugh!

Take a minute to go back and skim over each chapter. Do you remember some strategies speaking to your soul…and others, not so much?

Trust what your soul tells you and focus ONLY on the activities you're really excited about. Make a list of them and ignore the rest, for now anyway.

Choose one, two or maybe even three "new" strategies from your list. Three is actually fairly ambitious—most of these activities will require a fair amount of commitment from you, and I don't want you to overwhelm yourself unnecessarily and burn out on me!

Jennifer's $0.02

Do any of the chapters describe activities you're already doing, but you like the Prospect with Soul approach better? That's great! You probably already have many of the pieces and parts in place, so it may not be much work at all to tweak your approach to a more soulful one. For example, perhaps you hold a lot of open houses, but haven't been successful getting your guests to sign in, thus providing their contact information. Taking what you learned in Chapter Eight, you could try not asking for contact information at all, but rather taking a more casual, helpful approach and waiting until it's obvious your visitor wants to hear from you again!

The next step is to spend some quality time figuring out what needs to happen in order to put your new prospecting plan into action.

For example, if you decide to add the pursuit of Expired Listings to your business model, you'll need to come up with a strategy to find them, contact them and convey that you're the best thing that could have happened to them. Your plan will likely include things like developing a mailing campaign, creating an expired-specific presentation, doing daily MLS research, finding sources of contact information and practicing role-playing your initial contact. You may consider purchasing a program for pursuing Expired Listings (I recommend Borino's Expired Plus www.expiredplus.com). You might consider my "SWS

Listing Analyzer for Expired Listings" program (www.swsstore.com). You might set aside some time every day for a few weeks to read what other agents who pursue Expired Listings do (just search "Expired Listings" on ActiveRain, www.activerain.com).

Or let's say you want to finally get serious about social media. You'll need to choose your venue(s), signup, create a profile, pic(k) a pic(ture)or two for your profile, learn your way around, find some friends/contacts/associates, commit an hour a day to it and away you go.

How about becoming a Master of Your Market? Woo hoo—let's go look at houses!

Wanna reconnect with your sphere of influence? Make a list of everyone you know and, well, start reconnecting! (Okay, there's much more to it than that, but you know what I mean.)

Whatever you do, don't get so excited about your prospecting plan that you abandon your current clients. Remember, the very best way to ensure a consistent pipeline throughout your real estate career is to take great care of those who have already honored you with their real estate business.

Speaking of this, hopefully one of the prospecting activities that spoke to your soul was to provide exceptional customer service. That opens up a whole 'nother can of worms (in the nicest sense of those words) of creating your own systems and procedures and protocols for being a fabulous real estate agent. For help doing just that, I'll refer you to my listing agent-specific blog: www.selling-your-listings.com and my second book, FUN.

Remember in the beginning of this book where I assured you that you don't have to prospect for business in ways that make you feel icky? Just wanna repeat that here in case you missed it the first time. Never, ever sell your soul to be successful. You don't have to. I promise.

"I believe that being successful means having a balance of success stories across the many areas of your life. You can't truly be considered successful in your business life if your home life is in shambles."

Zig Ziglar

IN CONCLUSION...

Two Successful Careers...Two Vastly Different Approaches

IN the summer of 2008 (smack in the middle of the recession), I had an interesting conversation with a real estate agent who started in the business the same year I did, and we both worked for the same franchise. That first year, he was the Rookie of the Year...and I was runner-up to him. Neither of us recalls who was third, of course!

Anyway, we literally hadn't run into each other since that awards ceremony in the mid-90's. Oh, I'd seen his name around and he'd seen mine, but we'd never actually talked. We both went on to have successful careers and to set our individual worlds on fire (in our own minds anyway) and were both still alive and kicking, more than a dozen years later. Good thing.

So we had the opportunity to chat about our respective careers. Since his father had been a mega-producing broker at the time this guy (let's call him Skip) entered the business, I always assumed that Skip's success had been handed to him. Au contraire!

Skip explained that his dad wouldn't even let him in the door of his real estate office until he had, get this, worked for a year as a copier salesman. After that, he had to get his appraiser's license. Only then did Dad allow him to hang his new real estate license.

But that was only the beginning—the boot camp was next. Skip had to call all 600 of his dad's past clients, had to knock on 20 FSBO doors and call 20 Expired Listings per week. He had to hold two open houses every single Saturday.

And, voila! Skip was Rookie of the Year!

At the same time, I was taking my friends to lunch and attending social events with my future-ex-husband. I did some open houses and returned phone calls in nanoseconds. That was about it for me.

And voila! I was the Rookie of the Year Runner-up!

Truth be told, Skip blew me away in production. He sold 70 houses that first year to my 25. But I was pretty darn happy with my 25 and I was enjoying the heck out of my new real estate career. So, for me, it worked. Had I been forced thru Skip's boot camp, I wouldn't have made it past my first month.

Fast forward to that day we finally reconnected.

Both Skip and I had successful careers. We made a lot of money and were consistently top producers in our offices. I'm sure he had a lot of plaques on his "me wall," as did I.

But our approaches were still vastly different. He said he had to sell at least 100 houses a year to be profitable—that is, to support the systems and staff he'd put in place. He HAD to cold call, he HAD to door knock, he HAD to prospect, prospect, prospect to stay afloat. He said that if he only had 5 closings one month, he'd be in deep financial doo-doo.

As I spoke with Skip (who was seriously stressed out by the declining market), I was grateful that my business was very simple (and cheap) to run. It was just me, myself and I. No assistants, no buyer agents, not even a free-lance transaction coordinator. I didn't advertise, farm or SEO. Due to my strong sphere of influence, I had a steady stream of good business. Did I sell 100 houses that year? Uh, no. But did I work 60 hours a week? Nope. Not often, anyway.

I imagine Skip's annual income was close to a million, if not more. Mine? Nowhere close to a million! But did I feel as if I'd been blown away by my fellow Rookie? Not really.

I don't ever want to be in the position of having to be a mega-producer in order to survive. I just want to take on the amount of business I can handle all by myself, the amount of business that I can easily attract using the soulful methods and philosophies that have always worked for me.

So, Can a Real Estate Agent Who Prospects with Soul Be a Superstar?

Maybe, maybe not. Does that answer surprise you?

What does being a Superstar mean to you? And why, exactly, would you want to be one?

In my real estate market, the city's Superstar mega-producers sell hundreds of homes a year and make hundreds of thousands, strike that, millions of dollars a year. Bully for them. No hard feelings; they obviously have worked hard for their success and I don't begrudge them for it.

But neither do I want it.

So, if your question is, "Can I be among the heavy-hitters in my market even if I'm a Soulful Prospector?" then my response to you may very well be, "No, I don't think you can."

Why? Because in order to keep up with the seriously heavy-hitters in your marketplace, you're either

- working your backside off—like 20 hours a day (which leaves very little time for relationship-building and is likely a pace you can't keep up forever), and/or
- surrounded by a team of assistants (which gets in the way of creating that special bond between you and your clients) and/or
- doing a lousy job for those hundreds or thousands of clients.

But again, there's plenty of room on the planet for all different types of business-building strategies. If your goal is to be at the tippy-top of your profession—from a production standpoint—you will probably sacrifice some of the good will you might otherwise have developed with your clients. However, your trade-off will be the respect and admiration of your peers and of course, a steady stream of juicy paychecks. Nothing wrong with that!

Now, if by "Superstar" you simply mean that you're making good money and are maybe the top producing agent in your office or even just the Agent of the Month occasionally, then you can certainly reach Superstar status as a Soulful Prospector!

Why might you want to be a Superstar? In my case, I'm an egomaniac and I enjoy the heck out of being the Best in Office. I dig it. I have a "me" wall in my office that's covered with the plaques I've earned thru the years for my production. I'm proud of my success.

And yeah, well, I like the money, too.

But I never made $1M in one year selling real estate and I doubt I ever will. Can you imagine how hard you'd have to work to bring in a million bucks in twelve months selling real estate? To what end?

But if you visit most real estate training sites, you'll pretty quickly see references to being a Superstar or a Champion or a Hero or a Top Producer or some other high-falutin' descriptive term for a tippy-top level of real estate production. You'll see testimonials from agents who bought whatever system is being marketed claiming to have tripled their income or hit the half-million mark in commissions or sold 167 houses their first month on the program.

Wow. That's something. I'll admit to being intimidated by such marketing, both as a real estate agent and a real estate trainer myself. Gee, I never made $500,000 or sold 300 houses in a year. Neither has anyone I've ever coached or mentored or trained.

Do I believe the claims? Sure I do—no real reason to believe that such levels aren't attainable just because I never did it or know anyone who did.

But I don't believe that the majority of agents are going to see anywhere near those production levels, regardless of what system, program or philosophy they follow. No, not even in a good market.

And that's okay! I have a loyal following of several thousand real estate agents who don't want or need to set the world on fire—they just want to make a consistent, comfortable living, doing business in a manner they're proud of, making more people happy than unhappy. They also want to have time for their families, their hobbies and their naps. They don't want to be Power Prospectors who generate business 14 hours a day and then hand it off to their harem of assistants and specialists on their way out the door to drum up even more.

Hey, there's nothing wrong with wanting to be the Top Dog in your office, neighborhood, city, county or state. But if you don't, that's okay, too. There's plenty of room (and commission checks) here in the middle for those with slightly less-grand aspirations.

So, don't fret if you doubt you'll ever be a Superstar. You're in very good company. Just go forth, my friend…and have some fun…and sell some real estate. With Soul.

Appendix

"The Seduction of Your SOI," is an excerpt from "If You're Not Having Fun Selling Real Estate…"

The Seduction of Your Sphere of Influence

"You've achieved success in your field when you don't know whether what you're doing is work or play."

Warren Beatty

If you, like me, shudder at the thought of thickening your skin, playing the Numbers Game and scheduling at least three hours a day to ~~pester people~~ prospect, I have great news for you. You don't have to! There is a whole community of people out there, some of them you already know; many you don't (yet), ready and willing to send business and referrals your way!

In real estate, we call this community your Sphere of Influence (SOI) and it includes your friends, your family, your acquaintances, your friends' friends, your friends' families, your family's friends and your family's families. Every living, breathing person you know (or will know) has the potential to become your biggest cheerleader and to bring business your way without you even asking for it.

Your own personal Sphere of Influence can be responsible for most or even all of your business, if you approach it right. However, if your SOI strategy includes any sort of pestering, obligating or generally making a nuisance of yourself, not only will the business model fail, but you'll probably lose some friendships in the process.

Rest assured, I won't let you do that. Just keep reading.

Seduction?

When you saw the title of this chapter, did you wonder why on earth I used the term "seduction" in conjunction with generating business and referrals from the people who know you?

Oh, lots of reasons. First, I like it because it's fun, it's sexy, it's provocative and it grabs your attention. Having been single at various stages of my adult life, I also tend to see lots of analogies between the dating world and the business one, (keep reading; you'll find more). But on a deeper level, the term "seduction" is quite appropriate. While it may have negative connotations for some, overall, I think it's quite a positive word. Personally, I LOVE to be seduced, don't you?

Even when I'm aware I'm being seduced, I certainly enjoy the ride. I mean, if I were married and my husband came home tonight and outright announced he was expecting some action, I might be put off by his approach. I might feel a little used. However, if he came home with roses, gave me a big hug and kiss, helped me clear the table and then took out the trash, his chances of getting lucky would dramatically increase, wouldn't they? So what if I know what he's up to?

Or imagine a young man takes a young woman out on a date. If he were to ask her up front if he's going to get lucky that night, she would probably be offended, even though it's likely she realizes it's in the back of his mind. So, the smart young man takes a different approach. He is charming. He is friendly. He is appreciative. He is attentive. He is complimentary. He is respectful. In short, he's good company and makes her feel special.

Will his seduction efforts pay off? Who knows? But he's sure a whole lot closer than if he had just announced his intentions upfront. Again, the young woman probably knows she's being "seduced," but she's enjoying it.

So, let's compare a romantic seduction to the process of seducing your Sphere of Influence. Fact is you want something from your SOI. You want their business and referrals. You want to be invited to their parties. You want to be their favorite real estate agent, don't you?

Well, you could always call up everyone you know and tell them, couldn't you? Remind them on the first Monday of each month that You HEART Referrals!? Ask them if they know of anyone needing your services this week? Maybe even ask them for an invitation to their next social gathering?

But do you think they'd look forward to hearing from you? Do you think they'd appreciate your approach? Probably not; in fact, they might start avoiding your calls.

Conversely, what if you were to call up your friends every month or two and ask how they're doing and really listen? Maybe even offer to help or send out periodic informative emails or newsletters of interest to them instead of all about you. What if you invited your friends to your Super Bowl party or sent them a postcard from your vacation in Cancun?

Would your friends realize you want their business and referrals? Maybe, but they won't care—you are making them feel special and cared about.

Seduction works in a romantic arena; it also works in a prospecting one. If we are charming, friendly, appreciative, attentive, complimentary, respectful and fun to be around (and also reliable and competent), we'll get our friends' business and referrals. We don't have to beg for it; we really don't even need to ask for it.

(RE)Defining SOI

When I ask real estate agents to define what Sphere of Influence means to them, I typically get one of two responses—either: "Everyone I know" or "My Friends, Family and Past Clients."

Close, but not quite right.

To assume that your SOI is made up of Everyone You Know is dangerous and will lead you to a false sense of security (or, conversely, a false sense of rejection—see below). The problem is that in order for someone to be considered SOI, for business purposes anyway, they need to know two things about you. WHO you are and WHAT you do. Don't laugh! The people in our lives aren't keeping track of us on a regular basis, and if they haven't heard from us in awhile, they may very well have forgotten we exist or, at least, forgotten our occupation.

I once worked with a 3rd year real estate agent named Laurie. Laurie contacted me for help generating more business. When I suggested we approach her Sphere of Influence, she immediately objected, claiming that she'd already done that and that her SOI had never sent her any business. I convinced her to trust me, and we crafted an interesting, relevant, non-salesy reconnection letter and followed it up with an interesting, relevant, non-salesy email. Lo and behold, the vast majority of Laurie's SOI had no idea she was still selling real estate, and the calls of good wishes and support came flooding in. Within a month, Laurie had three new clients from her SOI.

At the other extreme, "My friends, family and past clients" is way too limiting. Unless you just got to town yesterday, you know a whole lot more people than that, and every single person you know has the potential to bring or send business your way. Just because someone isn't a best friend doesn't mean they won't be your biggest fan.

So, what's my definition of Sphere of Influence?

"Everyone Who Knows You and Knows that You Sell Real Estate"

When you see it in black and white, it seems obvious, doesn't it?

Okay, So WHO Is Your SOI?

Let's start with the obvious suspects. Your friends, family, current clients, past clients, current prospects and past prospects. Don't forget about your spouse's family, your spouse's work associates, your dog-groomer, your house-cleaner, the nurse at your chiropractor's office, your Spanish tutor, your pest-control guy, your renters and your landlord.

Never discount someone because you can't imagine they would ever have a need for you; you never know who they know and what social or professional circles they run around in. They might just be married to, best friends with or chiropractor to your biggest client ever!

Your SOI also potentially includes everyone you meet in your day-to-day wanderings. No, you don't have to (nor should you) accost everyone who crosses your path, but if you're open to friendly encounters with strangers, you'll be surprised how many new friends you can make in a week. What if you met one new person every day? Or even one a week?

How Many in Your SOI?

Shoot for an SOI of around 200 warm bodies, although more is perfectly fine. As we'll discuss shortly, you aren't depending on your 200 friends to hire you; you're actually not even after their business, although you'll certainly take it. No, your 200 friends are the gatekeepers to thousands of potential clients for you, both directly from their enthusiastic referrals, and indirectly through your social encounters with them.

What's so special about 200? Well, I'd like to blow you away with some complicated, yet oh-so-sensible mathematical formula to explain why 200 is the magic number, but I can't, really. It's just been my experience (and, frankly, a gut feeling) that if there are 200 people in the world who know who you are and know what you do, then that's enough to: 1) spread the word about your fabulousness, and 2) offer you enough social opportunities to spread the word yourself.

How Much Business Does Your SOI Have to Give?

One of the first objections real estate agents raise when presented with the idea of depending on one's SOI for business is that "I don't know anyone who wants to buy or sell a house right now! What if none of my friends has a real estate need? What then?"

Great question! However, as we alluded to above, you're not depending on your SOI to spoon-feed you their business—that would be a lousy business model. No, you're depending on your SOI to offer you opportunities to get your smiling face in front of everyone they know—either literally, with personal introductions, or figuratively with their referrals. This does not mean that you will need to bombard your SOI with aggressive sales pitches, or become a pest at their parties (if you do, you'll soon enough find yourself no longer invited!), but rather that you nurture the relationships you have with the intent of being someone your friends trust, like and are proud to be associated with.

There's a big difference.

Anyway, back to the question, "How much business does my SOI have to give me?"

Let's do some simple math.

If you know just 50 people on this planet, and all 50 of those people know 50 other people, that's a pool of over 2,000 potential clients for you. And what if those 2,000 each know 50 people? What if you know 100 people? 200 people? The numbers add up quickly.

Or how 'bout this? What if everyone you know knows just one person who will have a use for your real estate expertise this year? I think that's probably a reasonable expectation, so your goal is to become the go-to real estate agent in your social circles. And it's much easier than you might think to become that person.

The people you know have the potential to generate tons and tons of business for you, as long as you approach them, and their social network, correctly.

So how do you do that? It's pretty easy, actually—much easier and more common-sensical than most SOI trainers will have you believe.

Attracting Business to You

If you love being a real estate agent and you know your market, you'll attract business left and right, as long as you're out there in the world with your antenna up and a smile on your face. You don't need to shove your business card at everyone you meet, or dazzle them with a fantastic elevator speech—no, if your enthusiasm and expertise shine through in your casual conversations, the people you know and the people you meet will want to do business with you, if they have business to do.

So, the trick is to always be doing a couple of things:

First, always be mastering your market. The more intelligently you can speak about the local real estate market, the more magnetic you'll be when you're talking to people. For example, when I'm invited to a party, I try to check out the market in the area of the party ahead of time so that when I'm mingling at the party, if the subject of real estate comes up, I can talk about that house down the block that's been on the market for 9 months, and I know why it hasn't sold. I also know about the one around the corner that just came on the market last week. Even if I don't use the knowledge I obtained during my pre-party previewing, karma seems to work with me and will put me in a position to use it soon.

Seriously, a real estate agent who knows his market exudes a confidence that will draw people to him.

The second thing to be doing is related to the first, in that you should always be looking for opportunities to put your smiling face and your market expertise in front of other people. Now when I say this, I don't mean that you should make a nuisance out of yourself in public on a regular basis—do that and you might find yourself avoided—but rather open up room in your calendar for casual socializing. Accept invitations you might normally decline. Make a concerted effort to go to lunch with friends two or three times a week. Pick up the phone to ask a friend a question instead of shooting off an email. Go into the bank instead of the drive-thru.

The $10,000 Paycheck

You know what I love about this business? Every single person you meet every single day has the potential to bring you a $10,000 paycheck. And you have no idea who that person will be—it could be your mailman, it could be your hairdresser, it could be your dog-sitter. It could be the lady you sat next to at the nail salon. Every time you venture out into the world with your antenna up and a smile on your face, you could meet your next biggest client.

But, that probably won't happen if, when you venture out into the world you don't come across to people as someone who loves and is good at her job. And that's not the impression you leave when you're always in sales-pitch mode. So, leave the sales pitch at home, focus on being a great real estate agent who loves her job and knows her market and stays in touch with the people she knows without ever pestering them for business and referrals. I think you'll find that you'll attract far more business than you have in the past, and have a heck of a lot more fun doing it.

Is SOI Enough?

As of this writing, the real estate industry is suffering. In many markets, it seems that qualified buyers are non-existent, although there are plenty of motivated sellers. Unfortunately, it's tough to put a real estate deal together when the playing field is so lopsided!

I'm fortunate that my market in Denver, Colorado is fairly stable. We do have buyers for good properties, although nowhere near the volume of boom years past. In the good old days, just about everyone was in the real estate market, considering getting into the real estate market or knew someone who was. Therefore, it was like shooting fish in a barrel to find prospects for yourself—all you had to do was show up in public and you were surrounded by them! My first year as a real estate agent, I implemented a take-a-friend-to-lunch campaign that was wildly successful. Literally every time I went to lunch with a friend I walked away with a good lead that quite often led to a closing. Sweeeet. I thought I was pretty darn smart.

Well, in today's market, I could take-a-friend-to-lunch every day for a month and quite possibly walk away with nothing more than an extra ten pounds and a big Visa bill. Because my friends don't like me anymore? Not at all. Because they truly don't know anyone who needs a real estate agent. For many reasons, people are staying put right now.

So, in this world, "traditional" SOI, where you seduce your friends and send them out into the world to be your marketing department is not enough. Perhaps when good times return, it will be enough, but today…eh…not so much.

But does this mean that I'll have to resort to Old School real estate prospecting techniques like cold-calling, door-knocking, geographic farming (mass-mailing) or online marketing? Not at all (thank God).

It means that I'll need to take more responsibility for getting my smiling face and RCHB message in front of as many people as I can, with the intent of impressing as many as I can. (Basically, I need to expand my SOI on a darn near daily basis because there simply isn't the volume of business out there for the pickins.

"But Everyone I Know Already Knows Five Real Estate Agents!"

I'm certainly not the only sales trainer on the planet who espouses an SOI business model—there are a lot of us out there. Most have distinctly different philosophies from mine; in fact, many of my students appear on my virtual doorstep after trying these other methods and realizing they're not a good fit.

And that's fine, of course. As I said earlier, there are many paths to success, and mine is only one of them.

A common principle in many relationship-based approaches is that you should categorize your SOI based on the likelihood that they will generate business for you. It is recommended that in order to determine someone's category, you should outright ask that person if he or she is willing to refer real estate business to you. Your "A" group is made up of people who would most certainly be a business or referral source; someone who might refer would be a "B," and "C" is someone who probably won't. As you can imagine, your prospecting efforts with each category vary in intensity. You'll hit those A's hard; the B's sort of hard and pretty much ignore the C's. I've even seen some in my industry (who are rather too full of themselves, in my humble opinion), claim that they fine-tune their categories based on the number of times someone has referred! Until someone has performed for you at least ten times, they are not entitled to the honor of being in your "A" group.

Blech.

Besides, it's really dumb.

Here's the thing. Referral patterns can and do change. And y'know what? You have the power to change those patterns, starting today. There may be a whole bunch of people in your SOI who probably wouldn't hire you or refer to you today, but they might tomorrow or next month, as you change your behavior toward them. However, if you were to implement a policy of treating them according to your expectation that they'll hire or refer you, you've almost certainly cemented their position in your Category C group (which is not where you want them).

I change my opinions of the people in my world all the time, both positively and negatively. You probably do, too. Someone I thought walked on water two years ago might have hurt my feelings and is now off my radar. Someone who I barely gave a thought to might have done something really nice for me and is now my go-to source for whatever it is they do. Two years ago, I may have had no need for a financial planner, but today, with all the money I'm making from selling this book (!), I'm in desperate need of someone to manage my millions ;-].

One last thought on the topic of "But everyone I know already knows five other real estate agents."

In my world, it's a safe assumption that I'm not the only real estate agent my SOI knows. I may very well be one of five or ten or even more. 'Specially during boom times, it seems that every other warm body on the planet has a real estate license and would sure like to do something with it (that is, sell a house and get a paycheck).

However, I've never felt in competition with the thousands of other real estate agents in my community, even if they're friends of my friends. Why? Because I'm better than they are (the other agents, that is). And not only am I better than my competition, I'm way better at staying in touch with my SOI. Now that's a rare combination—a great real estate agent who does a great job of staying in touch. I'm serious—if you do both, you'll have no problem filling your pipeline and keeping it full. It really is (almost) that simple.

Is SOI Right for You?

While a Sphere of Influence business model can be a beautiful alternative to the more traditional methods of pursuing business, it's not right for everyone.

SOI Will Work for You If...

- You are darn good at being a real estate agent, and
- The people you know perceive you to be a Reasonably Competent Human Being, and
- You know people, or are willing to meet some, and
- You take good care of your clients, and
- You enjoy what you do.

SOI May Not Work for You If...

- You aren't darn good at selling real estate, or
- The people you know think you're a flake, or
- You don't know anyone and like it that way, or
- You'd rather hunt for new clients than take care of the ones you have, or
- You're unhappy with your career path.

1. Are you really good at managing a real estate transaction? As we just discussed, you need to be refer-worthy to succeed with your Sphere of Influence. If your past clients wouldn't use you again and don't recommend you to others, you'll always have to be on the prowl for new clients. If you don't take good care of the referrals you receive from your friends, those referrals will eventually stop coming in. Which is not only bad for business, it's also bad for your friendships.

2. Are you an RCHB (a Reasonably Competent Human Being)? If your friends perceive you to be a generally reliable, ethical, organized, dependable person, they'll be delighted to send business your way, even if they have no personal experience with your service. However, if your social circle sees you as a bit of a flake, you may have some repair work to do before you'll see much success with your SOI.

3. Do you have a reasonably robust circle of friends or acquaintances, or are you willing to pursue one? Depending on one's Sphere of Influence requires that one has a Sphere of Influence. That is—that you know people. It doesn't mean that you must have a wide circle of friends, but it is necessary that there are people in your community who know who you are! If this is not the case today, are you willing to make an effort to change that?

4. Are you committed to taking great care of your current clients? If you make taking care of your current clients your priority, they will take care of you the rest of your days. However, if you focus your efforts more on pursuing tomorrow's business than taking care of today's, it doesn't matter how "good"

you are at your job; your clients won't feel loved…and will express that sentiment in their referral patterns!

5. Do you enjoy what you do? Do you really? There's something magical about sincere enthusiasm. When someone loves their job, you almost can't help but want to work with them—it's magnetic. And y'know what? If you radiate enthusiasm about what you do, others will assume that you're good at what you do. Sweeeet.

Creating an SOI Business Model

I teach an eight-week course called "The Savvy Prospector," where we go through the entire process of creating a Sphere of Influence business model from scratch. You can visit my website to learn more (www.sellwithsoul.com). But here's a quick summary of the process.

It's not rocket science, but it can be a bit labor intensive upfront. Getting an SOI business model up and running takes about a month and includes the following steps:

- Make a list of everyone you know and enter it into a contact management system
- Write an interesting, relevant, non-salesy announcement or reconnection letter to everyone on your list
- Create an SOI business plan and set goals
- Implement your plan

Step One

The first step—making a list of everyone you know—is probably something you have done at least once in your career. Whether or not you've kept up that list is another story. Most agents don't, so if you haven't, don't feel bad. However, that list is a gold mine for you, especially if you keep it updated. In fact, if you make your list and keep it maintained through the years, you may never have to prospect for business again.

As you're putting together your very first list, or reorganizing the one you have, you will probably notice that there are two general categories of contacts in your

Sphere, the first being those in your social network and the second being, well, everyone else who knows you and knows that you sell real estate. The first group, which I call (very cleverly) my Group One, is made up of the people I'd probably invite to my wedding. The "everyone else" group, which I call Group Two, includes clients, prospects, work associates, service providers—anyone I don't necessarily consider a "friend," but who would recognize my name if I called them up. I define my Group One as those I'd be comfortable asking out for coffee; my Group Two are those I wouldn't. But don't underestimate the power of your Group Two—just because someone isn't your best friend doesn't mean they don't respect your abilities as a real estate agent. I get a lot of business from my Group Two.

Step Two

The second step, writing your reconnection letter, can be a turning point in your career, as long as your letter is interesting, relevant and non-salesy. If you use one of the boiler-plate, corporate-inspired (or referral-begging based) letters, you'll be wasting your time, money and energy.

Even if you've been around the real estate block a time or two, that's no excuse to bore your readers to death. Believe me, our friends have lots and lots of choices when it comes to real estate agents. Don't count on their loyalty just because you send them boring, scripted letters on a regular basis thanking them for their support and begging for their referrals.

Most real estate agents have great personalities that shine through when they speak out loud. But put them in front of a keyboard or hand them a pen and paper...and apparently they freeze up. At least, that's how it seems when I read the nonsense they create when communicating in written form.

There's no reason your written communication should be any less exciting and interesting than you are in person. Even if you aren't the world's most gifted writer, that's no excuse. If you can speak intelligently and usually hold your listener's interest, then you can transfer that ability to paper.

Step Three

The next step is to create a business plan for yourself. Now, don't worry. It's not complicated or complex or tedious; it'll probably take you less than an hour to do. All you need to do is sit down and think of activities you enjoy that include people you already know or increase the likelihood that you'll meet new people. And then decide how many times a week, a month, a quarter or a year you're doing to do these activities.

For example, here are some items you might include:

- Lunch/coffee/margarita/dinner dates
- Personal emails
- Collecting business cards
- Floor time
- Mass emails
- Thank you cards
- Blog about your neighborhood
- Go to the office
- Attend PTA meetings

- Personal phone calls
- Handing out business cards
- Adding names to your SOI
- Monthly get-togethers
- Postal mailings
- Join a new group
- Get Out There in the World
- Open houses
- Attend neighborhood meetings

Next, you put the activities into a simple spreadsheet and create goals for yourself as to frequency.

Here's an excerpt from my own SOI business plan:

ACTIVITY	TARGET AUDIENCE	GOAL
Lunch/coffee/dinner date	Group One	2 per week
Personal phone calls	Group One	2 per week
Personal emails	Group One	3 per week
Monthly get-together	Group One	1 per month
Add names to SOI	Groups One and Two	3 per week
Mass emails	Groups One and Two	1 per month
Postal mailings	Groups One and Two	2 more this year
Thank you cards	Anyone	3 per week
Join a "group"	n/a	1 per month
Attend a community event	n/a	2 per month
Hand out business cards	Anyone	5 per day
Collect business cards	Anyone	1 per day

Step Four

Once you've made your list and sent out your letter to everyone on your list and created your business plan, it's time to implement that plan.

It's pretty easy—just follow the plan! Schedule lunch dates, look for opportunities to pick up the phone and call people you know (without a hint of a sales pitch), spend half an hour every morning sending out personal emails. Keep your antenna up for opportunities to thank people. Think of creative ways to hand out your business card without being a pest about it. Accept invitations to parties and have a few of your own. Go inside the bank instead of through the drive-thru. When you're at Walmart, smile at people instead of avoiding eye-contact.

The good news is that after a month or two of consciously following your plan, you won't really need the plan anymore. You'll be doing it naturally and you'll be seeing results from it that will inspire you to keep it up. My SOI business plan pretty much runs itself so the only reminders I need at this point are to do my two-to-three-times-a-year postal mailings and my monthly mass emails. Otherwise, I just do this stuff naturally.

So, the big picture…if you are a great real estate agent who stays in touch with the people you know without ever making a nuisance of yourself, you're WAY ahead of your competition. Your competition is made up of other great real estate agents AND other real estate agents who stay in touch with their clients, but very few Great Agents Who Do a Good Job of Staying in Touch.

Contributors

A big THANK YOU to everyone who contributed their brilliance to *Prospect with Soul!* The book wouldn't have been the same without you, that's for sure.

Janie Coffey

Janie has always been a gracious contributor to my books, programs and products and I hope she knows how much I appreciate her! She is an equestrian specialist and has a uniquely insightful grasp of the power of social media. Janie has been a SWS'er from the start and practices the Golden Rule in her real estate business. If you need someone genuinely soulful to refer to in South Florida – talk to Janie. You can find her at www.thecoralgablesstory.com.

Dennis J. Giannetti

Dennis is SWS's new best friend! He has a passion for taking the soulful message to the masses, and the talent, expertise and work ethic to get it done. We're pretty excited about the future around here, and Dennis figures to be a big part of it. He is the Regional Vice President and Chief Learning Officer for Illustrated Properties in South Florida (www.ipre.com) and has worked as an agent, manager, coach and trainer in the real estate industry since 1990. Dennis holds a Masters degree in conflict resolution and a second masters in training and development and believes that real estate agents can "increase the balance in their checkbook and their lives" by knowing who they are and bringing that uniqueness to what they do.

Susan Haughton

I've always described Susan as my "Soul Sister" and, well, nothing has changed since the last time I said that! Except that I enjoy her friendship and admire the way she runs her business more than ever. Susan raised eyebrows during her rookie year when she refused to prospect for business in the traditional manner expected of new agents...and then surprised 'em all when she won the Rookie of the Year award in her office. Susan works in Old Town Alexandria, Virginia and has been a member of the Long & Foster's Chairman's Club since 2005. She's an insightful and entertaining blogger; check her out at www.activerain.com/blogs/susanmovesyou.

Matt Jones

My good friend Matt Jones really "gets" Selling and Prospecting with Soul. We've had many entertaining conversations about the ridiculousness of some of our industry's sacred cows, and I always come away from our talks with one or two fun "aha!" epiphanies, and I dare say he does as well. Matt is the is the founder and CEO of FavoriteAgent.com and a nationally syndicated author of nearly a dozen books for real estate agents. Matt's North Carolina-based company has been profiled by major media outlets as an innovator and a pioneer in the industry, and CNN's Pulse on America claimed FavoriteAgent.com to be "changing the way real estate is being done in America." To learn more about Matt, visit his website at www.LCMsuccess.com, or his blog at www.blogmattblog.com.

Lisa Petersen

I always enjoy hearing from Lisa Petersen, one of my long time readers. I know when I see her name in my inbox, there will be something of value to read and quite possibly to file away in my little stash of SWS'er brilliance. Lisa is a real estate broker in Vancouver, Washington with 20 years experience in a wide variety of real estate-related ventures. If you're looking for a solid agent to refer to in the Vancouver area, give Lisa a shout. Her website is www. DLPHomes.com. I'm sure she'd love to hear from you!

Erica Ramus

Erica is the broker/owner of Realty Executives in Pottsville, Pennsylvania and one of my go-to resources when I need intelligent discussion on one of my tele-seminar shows! Erica is an impressive woman in the real estate world – she's one of ActiveRain's top bloggers, a contributor to Agent Genius, and has been profiled in REALTOR Magazine. In 2008 she was named one of Northeast Pennsylvania's "Top 20 Business Women." I'm proud to count Erica among my readers...and my friends. You can learn more about Erica (and say hello!) at www.schuylkillrealestate.com.

Bob Stewart

When I called up ActiveRain's "Chief Evangelist" Bob Stewart and asked for some material about blogging for my little book, he immediately offered to help. Yay! I'm a huge fan of ActiveRain and of Mr. Stewart, so it's an honor to include his wisdom here. Bob is responsible for growing and maintaining the ActiveRain community of real estate professionals and has been at the helm of the community as their membership has skyrocketed from 8,000 in 2006 to over 200,000 (and counting) in 2011. If you aren't already a member of ActiveRain, you should definitely consider joining the fun today, at www.ActiveRain.com.

Resources

Free Stuff at SellwithSoul.com

Like any good website, we offer lots of free stuff…to draw you in, get you addicted and then sell you all our goodies…well, that's the plan anyway! But whether or not you ever buy anything from us, we thought you might like to know what's there for the taking.*

FREE NEWSLETTERS

- The Daily Seduction—Tips & Strategies for Generating Business & Referrals from the Very Important People Who Know You (Your Sphere of Influence)
- The Reluctant Prospector—Sanity Savers for Introverts & Other Reluctant Prospectors
- Confidence-Builders for Rookie Real Estate Agents

LOUNGES & FORUMS

- The VIP Lounge—This is where you'll find checklists, a sample listing presentation, sample client communications, vendor recommendations & more
- The Sell with Soul Forum—Where the smartest, coolest, funniest people in real estate hang out

---

* These offerings are subject to change, of course.

TELESEMINAR TRAINING

At least twice a month we provide free teleseminar training in the SWS Virtual Studio. Details and registration are available at the SWS Calendar of Events.

Just visit www.SellwithSoul.com to access these resources.

Want More?

JENNIFER WRITES . . .

If you enjoyed *Prospect with Soul for Real Estate Agents* and want more, you're in luck! Jennifer loves to write, so you can find hours and hours of soulful material all over the WWW. Of course, you can purchase her first two books, *Sell with Soul: Creating an Extraordinary Career in Real Estate without Losing Your Friends, Your Principles or Your Self-Respect* and *If You're Not Having Fun Selling Real Estate, You're Not Doing It Right* on her website or at Amazon.com. But if you're not in the mood to spend your dollars today, here are some links to her free blogs and articles:

- www.RealtyTimes.com (just search for Jennifer Allan)
- www.SellwithSoulblog.com
- www.Sphere-of-Influence.com
- www.TheConfidentRookie.com

JENNIFER SPEAKS . . .

Yes, Jennifer writes about real estate, but she speaks about it, too! Out loud—to your office, group or association. Help us spread the word that there is an alternative to cheesy Old School tactics & techniques, that serving one's current clients is the highest and best use of a real estate agent's time and that it is possible to succeed in a real estate career without sacrificing one's soul to do so.

Jennifer speaks on a variety of topics, including "Selling to Your Sphere of Influence: No Sales Pitch Required," "For Sale Signs Don't Pay the Bills," "Selling Real Estate is Not a Numbers Game," and, of course, "Choosing the Right Prospecting Strategies for You."

To learn more or to request a proposal, visit www.SellwithSoul.com/jennifer-speaks.html.

JENNIFER COACHES . . .

Want to implement something you just read about in *Prospect with Soul?* Talk to Jennifer. Whether you're just starting out or taking it to the next level, she can help you figure out what to do now, what to do next, and what to do after that. She doesn't have a formal coaching program in place—and that's by design. She evaluates and advises each client as an individual, according to his or her personality, lifestyle, goals and budget. No long-term contracts or condescending sales pitches; just a sincere desire to help agents reach their goals—no matter how lofty or down-to-earth they may be.

Interested? Just contact Jennifer at Jennifer@sellwithsoul.com.

THE SWS REFERRAL NETWORK

So, after reading *Prospect with Soul,* do you think this is a philosophy you could embrace? If so, consider becoming a member of the SWS Referral Network, an exclusive group of agents who have committed to a higher level of service and expertise than your average real estate licensee.

Check us out at www.SellwithSoul.com/sws-referral-network.html.

Index

exceptional service; referral-based
business; taking care of clients

D

Davis, Sammy, Jr., 188
Days on Market (DOM), 86–87, 118
Daytimers, 170
desk duty. *See* floor time
direct SOI, 44
Disney, Walt, 209
DOM, 86–87, 118
Do Not Call (DNC) List, 163, 191, 193–94
doo-dads, 122–28
door-knocking, 13, 20, 81, 143, 190–98, 229
  Jennifer's Blog on, 196

E

elevator speeches, 34–36
emails
  mass, 114–18
  with online leads, 187
email signatures, 213
emotional maturity, 67
Envelope Addressing, Four Golden Rules of,
  121
exceptional service, 53, 206, 213. *See also*
  customer service; referral-based
  business; taking care of clients
expired listings, 156–59, 163–67, 215–16
extroverts, 23, 25

F

Facebook, 130–31, 168–71, 174–76
farming. *See* geographic farming
first impressions, 203
floor calls, 97
floor leads, seller, 98–99
floor time, 83, 85, 90–100, 147
follow-through, 67
follow-ups, post-closing, 204–5
For Sale By Owner (FSBOs), 20, 72, 143,
  156–63, 165–67, 210, 213
  Jennifer's Blogs on, 160, 165
Four Golden Rules of Envelope-Addressing,
  121
Franklin Planners, 170
FSBOs. *See* For Sale By Owner

G

Garland, Judy, 7
geographic farming, 143–55
  choosing the right approach, 152
  costs of, 150–51

getting the word out, 147–48
  intentional, 148–51, 154–55
  as neighborhood specialist, 146–47
  organic, 144–45, 152–54
Giannetti, Dennis J., 2–6, 238
Godin, Seth, 28
The Go-Giver (Burg and Mann), 70–72, 75
Go-Giver agents, 70–72, 75
Go-Givers Sell More (Burg and Mann), 11–12,
  70–72, 75
graphics design, 212
Guru.com, 142, 212

H

Haughton, Susan, 95–96, 239
helpfulness, 92. *See also* customer service;
  exceptional service
Hepp, Virginia, 134
ho-hum doo-dads, 124–25
holiday cards, 121

I

*If You're Not Having Fun Selling Real Estate,
  You're Not Doing it Right* (Allan), 26,
  41, 44, 95, 98, 216, 222–37, 242
impressing your clients, 201–8
incentives, 52–53
indirect SOI, 44–45
informational blog posts, 135
initial conversations with prospects, 90–100,
  114–18
intentional geographic farming, 148–51,
  154–55
Interludes
  Do You Believe in Your Product?, 197–98
  The Go-Giver Real Estate Agent, 70–72
  For Introverts Only, 23–25
  Is It Mercenary to Use Your Sphere of
    Influence for Business?, 80–81
Internet inquiries, 90, 99–100
Internet leads. *See* Online leads
Internet prospecting, 26
Interruption Marketing, 28. *See also*
  advertising
The Introvert Advantage (Laney), 24
introverts, 23–25
  Jennifer's Blog on, 123

J

Jennifer's Blog
  at ActiveRain, 130
  Can I Get One of Your Business Cards?,
    31